LAND ROVER

Other books by the author:

Key Facts Colour Guide – Photography
Take Better Pictures

LAND ROVER

SIMPLY THE BEST

Martin Hodder

Haynes Publishing

First published 1998

A catalogue record for this book is available from the British Library

ISBN 1 85960 437 4

Library of Congress catalog card number 98-72317

Haynes North America, Inc.,
861 Lawrence Drive, Newbury Park,
California 91320, USA.

Published by Haynes Publishing, Sparkford,
Nr Yeovil, Somerset BA22 7JJ, UK.

Tel: 01963 440635 Fax: 01963 440001
Int. tel: +44 1963 440635 Fax: +44 1963 440001
E-mail: sales@haynes-manuals.co.uk
Web site: http://www.haynes.com

Designed & typeset by
G&M, Raunds, Northamptonshire.
Printed and bound in Great Britain by
J. H. Haynes & Co. Ltd., Sparkford.

Note on imperial/metric conversions

Unless usually referred to only in metric units (eg engine capacity in cubic centimetres [cc] or litres [l]) or imperial units (eg carburettors in inches [in]), common measurements of length, area, volume, weight and speed in the text and specifications are given in imperial units with metric equivalents in parathenses, *except* in the following less common instances:

282 ÷ miles per gallon (mpg)
= litres per 100 kilometres (l/100km)

Torque:
pounds-force feet (lb/ft) x 0.113
= Newton metres (Nm)

Pressure:
pounds-force per square inch (psi) x 6.895
= Kilopascals (kPa)

Contents

Introduction

I have enjoyed a love affair with Land Rovers since I first sat in one in 1956. Just 16 years old, I was fully captivated by the square-cut appearance and functional simplicity of the new machine which a friend's father had just acquired for work on and around the farm he managed in Suffolk. My admiration of the Land Rover grew when I spent a year in South Africa in the early-1960s. Working for a daily newspaper in the Orange Free State, I sometimes came across hard-worked Land Rovers which made easy going of the vast landscape of the high veldt, on one occasion enjoying an extended trek over road-less countryside which no other vehicle, apart from tractors or all-wheel drive trucks, could have tackled.

Back in Britain I began competing in motorcycle trials. After one in Wales in the mid-1960s a friend demonstrated the off-roading ability of his Series II 88-inch pick-up by driving it up a rocky stream bed which had been used in the event. He invited me to have a go … and a passion for four-wheel off-roading was born.

Over the 30 years since then I have owned, or had the use of, a variety of Land Rovers, Range Rovers, and Discoverys, every one of which has given great joy, unrivalled satisfaction, and occasional heart-ache when things have gone expensively wrong. It was from this relationship with Land Rovers that this book was born. This is not intended as a work of history, nor is it a technical book, but rather it is a celebration of the Land Rover marque, in which I am happy to share with the reader my personal passion for the machinery of Solihull, a passion reflected in the massive enthusiast movement which has grown around these vehicles.

Many books have been written about Land Rovers down the years, a large number of them truly informative, especially those on the history of the marque penned by James Taylor. Mine makes no attempt to compete with works such as these, without which no Land Rover-owning home is complete; instead I have taken an individualistic approach to key aspects concerning the ownership and enjoyment of Land Rovers, including what is, in many ways, a fresh look at everything that has happened in the past to give us what we have today. In effect, this book is a mirror image of the Land Rover enthusiast movement, and the interests of the individuals within it. However, while writing it I have borne in mind that over recent years there has been an influx of new enthusiasts who are not necessarily highly-skilled home mechanics, or who are not yet deeply concerned with the nut-and-bolt detail of Series I or Series II Land Rovers.

The huge popularity of the Discovery has introduced a great many people to the fascination of Land Rovers and the enjoyment of off-roading, while the excellent value of Range Rovers built before, say, the end of the 1980s has opened the door for large numbers of families for whom their vehicle is a combination of weekday workhorse and weekend fun at minimal cost. It is specifically for such enthusiasts as these that parts of this book have been written. By explaining the different roles of the various modern, and relatively modern, machines and by providing frank descriptions of the abilities of each of them, I have tried to provide important information to those who want to purchase a Land Rover, but who may not be entirely sure which is the most suitable vehicle. Then there's the question of what to do with the Land Rover once it has been acquired. In providing a detailed analysis of the enthusiast movement, under the title 'Land Rovers at play', my aim is to give newcomers to Land Rovers a focal point for their interest. The importance of the 100-plus Land Rover clubs, along with the invaluable contribution of the specialist press and the successful *Land Rover Owner* Billing Show, are all charted.

Most people who have the use of Land Rovers will, at some time, want to try out their legendary off-road capabilities. The two big problems facing newcomers to the movement, along with many who have been around it for some time, are how to go about learning off-road driving techniques, and where to go off-road driving. This book doesn't attempt to tell its reader how to drive off-road, but it does provide general information on off-roading and worthwhile advice on how and where to learn.

Considerable coverage is also given to the role of the original Range Rover in the fortunes not only of Land Rover, but of the parent Rover company. The Range Rover is, in many ways, an unsung hero, and this is something I have attempted to redress, pointing out that without the success of the Range Rover the fortunes of Rover itself would have become decidedly shaky at times. The development of the Range Rover project from the mid-1960s through to its launch in 1970, and beyond, is told in the kind of detail which has not been seen before. This is not conventional history-telling, but an intimate, behind-the-scenes account which is revealing in the way it shows the project unfolding. To tell this story I interviewed at great length one of the key members of the project team, Geof Miller. Among the many tasty morsels revealed is the story of how Geof – the only member with a personal interest in Land Rovers and experience of off-roading – took the entire project team on an off-roading expedition so that they could understand what was required of an off-roading vehicle.

In a separate chapter I have looked at the story of the V8 engine, without which the Range Rover could never have been the success story it became. The way in which this engine, originally developed by Buick in the late-1950s, was discovered by Rover more or less by chance makes fascinating reading.

The book would not have been complete without the story of Land Rover's early days, starting with the development work which began on the original prototype in 1947. I have tried to pull together those aspects which most put the company's astonishing story into its remarkable perspective. And bringing the story of the utility Land Rovers fully up to date is the development of the present-day Defender since its birth in 1983, the ultimate machine for off-roading enthusiasts around the world. To come up with such an excellent vehicle would be considered inspirational by most manufacturers, but in the case of Land Rover it had a lot more to do with evolution, as my account shows.

The way in which Land Rovers have played a leading role in the majority of armies around the world makes a compelling chapter, even for people without the slightest interest in matters military. And as one of the few people to have driven many of the vehicles in the renowned Dunsfold Collection, I have been able to write in detail about the world's greatest museum of historically significant Land Rovers.

I make no apology for not even trying to disguise my own enthusiasm for everything to do with Land Rover, and consider it a privilege to have the opportunity to share that enthusiasm with you.

Martin Hodder
Towcester, 1998

Acknowledgements

Special thanks are due to Geof Miller for the time he made available for the detailed interviews on the development of the Range Rover and the inside story of the technical problems on the Trans Americas Expedition, and for the photographs he provided. Geof told me that he has been intending for years to write his own book on the Range Rover, but in the event he was pleased to relate the story to me.

The celebrated artist Pete Wilford volunteered to produce a special drawing for the book, and came up with an absolute gem which depicts Geof Miller working hard beneath a Range Rover in the Amazonian jungle during the Trans Americas trip.

Among the many others who provided assistance and information are Philip Bashall, David Mitchell, Vince Cobley, Richard Green, and Carl Rodgerson. And I owe a special vote of thanks to world-leading Rover historian James Taylor, whose highly informative articles and books I have read avidly for many years, and to military historian Bob Morrison, whose feature articles have done a great deal to open my eyes to the present-day relationship between Land Rover and its military users.

The photographs are from my own collection unless credited otherwise. The black-and-white historical shots and a few others were kindly provided by Jonathan Day at the National Motor Museum Photographic Library.

Finally, my thanks to Denis Chick and Mike Gould at Land Rover for their encouragement, assistance, and loan of vehicles, and to Darryl Reach of Haynes Publishing for making the whole thing possible.

Chapter One

The family of Land Rovers

There cannot be a motor manufacturer anywhere in the world who is not envious of Land Rover. And there is no group of users more enthusiastic about the vehicles they drive than Land Rover owners. The company goes from strength to strength, seemingly able to come up with world-beating models without effort time after time. And that, of course, does not happen by chance, no matter how easy the Solihull factory may make it appear.

Land Rover owes its success to a

The Land Rover stand at the Commercial Motor Show in 1956, reflecting the commercial nature of Land Rovers at the time. However, there was considerable choice, and this picture shows 86-inch and 107-inch hard-tops, station wagons, and soft-tops. (National Motor Museum)

In contrast to the early period, the greatest emphasis today is placed on providing a choice of models for the everyday motorist, with only the Defender 90 representing utility vehicles in the line-up depicted here. Nearest the camera is a three-door Freelander hard-top, with a five-door behind it, then a Range Rover, a Defender 90, and a Discovery.

number of key points: (1) Coming up with the right product in the first place; (2) Developing it through evolution, not revolution; (3) Retaining a family appearance; and (4) Having the right people doing the right jobs within the organisation. All of these factors combined have led to the comprehensive line-up which constitutes today's excellent range. In technical terms, ability, comfort, and usability they are far removed from the vehicles which began it all, 50 years ago, and yet there's a physical resemblance which is unmistakable. Even the Freelander, sleekest machine ever to wear the Land Rover name, possesses that all-important family resemblance and displays its lineage with pride.

No other motor manufacturer can even begin to approach Land Rover when it comes to offering such a comprehensive range of 4×4s. Whether you're looking for a working vehicle for farm or construction site, or a supremely luxurious machine whose off-roading ability may never be used in anger, but is there just in case, Land Rover has the vehicle for you. Each one has the same level of toughness as the working Defender, and they all (apart from the Freelander, which is a rather different concept) have exceptional off-roading capabilities, no matter how opulent the interior. Above all, they are Land Rovers, and that's what sets them apart from the crowd.

Defender

The Defender, which dates back in its original form to 1983, is the central pivot around which all other Land Rover vehicles revolve. Its ancestry goes directly back to the Series I, and the basic shape and design of the body have a quite remarkable resemblance to the Land Rovers of half a century ago. However, although the earlier models – Series I, II, IIA, and III – all had levels of competence which were unmatched in their day, the Defender's all-round ability is vastly superior to that of the Land Rovers from which it evolved. It is the ultimate workhorse, equally at home towing heavy trailers to market towns, ploughing through the deep mud of construction sites, or climbing mountain tracks in search of lost sheep or stranded hill-walkers.

There are no less than ten different types of Defender, with three wheelbases and five body types – hard-top, pick-up, station wagon, crew cab, and high-capacity pick-up. The wheelbases are 92.9in, 110in, and 127in. All Defenders (except USA-specification models) are powered with the superb Land Rover 300 Tdi turbo diesel engine, the best engine of its type ever produced and a perfect match for the working character of the vehicle. This 2.5 litre engine, also used in the Discovery, injects fuel directly into the combustion chamber, without the use of the pre-combustion chamber which is present in most diesels. The direct injection system produces more power and, at the same time, gives a 25–30 per cent fuel economy advantage. The 300 Tdi was redesigned from the earlier 200 Tdi, itself an excellent unit, and further advantages include reduced emissions when working in conjunction with the standard catalytic

This is the ultimate off-roading machine. Even with standard tyres and without special off-roading equipment, off the tarmac the Defender 90 cannot be beaten, yet is more than civilised enough to be used for long road journeys at motorway speeds.

Defender specifications

	90	110	130
Engine	2.5 litre 4-cylinder in-line turbo diesel direct injection		
Power	111.3bhp @ 4,000rpm		
Torque	195lb/ft @ 1,800rpm		
Transmission	5-speed permanent 4x4 with transfer box		
Suspension (front)	Live beam axle, coil springs, telescopic dampers, Panhard rod		
Suspension (rear)	Live beam axle, coil springs, telescopic dampers, A-frame		
Wheelbase	92.9in	110in	127in
Fuel capacity	12gal	17.5gal	17.5gal
Towing weight (with over-run brakes)	3,500kg	3,500kg	3,500kg
Ground clearance	7.5in (pick-up) 9in (hard-top/stn wgn)	8.5in	8.5in
Wading depth	20in	20in	20in
Max gradient	45°	45°	45°
Approach angle	48° (pick-up) 51.3° (hard-top)	50°	50°
Departure angle	49° (pick-up) 53° (hard-top)	34.3°	34°

NB Vehicle dimensions and weights vary according to body type

converter. The most noticeable characteristic of the Land Rover diesel engine is its exceptionally high torque figure of 195lb/ft (in some applications), which is produced at only 1,800rpm. It is this which makes the engine so suitable for towing heavy loads and for off-road operation. The 300 Tdi's maximum power is 111.3bhp, produced at 4,000rpm, and although this is a respectable figure, it is the torque which is more important in many Land Rover situations.

The second key aspect of the Defender's specification is its transmission, a five-speed permanent four-wheel drive arrangement combined with a transfer box, which has been developed over the years from the system first seen in the Range Rover in 1970. The transfer box enables a second, lower, set of gear ratios to be selected, giving the Defender amazing pulling power and the ability to negotiate the most difficult off-road obstacles. Because of the permanent four-wheel drive arrangement it is necessary to have, in addition to the normal differentials on both axles, a central differential which effectively splits the drive between front and rear axles, and protects the transmission from damage caused by 'wind-up' in everyday use. This centre differential can be locked, or engaged, in order to maximise tractive effort in particularly slippery conditions, such as when driving through mud or snow.

The next crucial component of the Defender is its suspension, again very closely related to the system pioneered for the original Range Rover. At its heart is the use of long-travel coil springs, providing exceptional wheel articulation, which, by maximising the contact between tyre and surface in extreme off-roading situations, is one of the keys to the Defender's unrivalled ability off the tarmac. Also important are the Defender's ground clearance, exceptional arrival and departure angles (especially in the 90), and its wading ability.

Discovery

To a large degree the Discovery was born from the Range Rover Classic, yet despite the close mechanical relationship, the Discovery has a style and character all of its own which has permitted it to slice right through the general purpose 4×4 market into a position of total dominance. It is a charismatic vehicle with a strong personality and toughness that belie its modern good looks. Launched at the Frankfurt Motor Show in September 1989, the vehicle went on to play a major part in Land Rover's success over the next nine years. Yet, in the best traditions of the company, it was in many ways more of an evolutionary development of the Range Rover than a truly new vehicle. It utilised the highly successful Range Rover chassis, suspension, and transmission, along with (if you wanted) its V8 petrol engine. But two aspects of the Discovery were totally new – the attractive body, and a breakthrough in engine design that was to prove highly significant. A completely new direct injection 2.5-litre diesel engine, the 200 Tdi, had been developed for the vehicle, and this was also destined to see service in the Range Rover before

The Discovery is the perfect compromise vehicle, offering excellent long-distance cruising, 30mpg economy (with the Tdi engine), and quite remarkable off-roading ability. In this shot the Discovery has just completed a near non-stop journey to the mountains of Southern Spain, without any discomfort.

Discovery specifications

Engine	2.5 litre 4-cylinder in-line turbo diesel direct injection/3.9 litre V8 petrol injection
Power (Tdi)	111.3bhp @ 4,000rpm/179.7bhp @ 4750rpm
Torque (Tdi)	195lb/ft @ 1,800rpm/229.5lb/ft @ 3,100rpm
Power (Tdi auto)	120bhp @ 4,000rpm
Torque (Tdi auto)	220.7lb/ft @ 2,000rpm
Power (V8)	164bhp @ 4,750rpm
Torque (V8)	212 @ 2,600rpm
Transmission	5-speed manual/4-speed automatic permanent 4x4 with transfer box
Suspension (front)	Live beam axle, coil springs, telescopic dampers
Suspension (rear)	Live beam axle, coil springs, telescopic dampers
Wheelbase	100in
Length	178in
Height	75in
Width	86in
Fuel capacity	19.5 gal
Towing weight (with over-run brakes)	3,500kg
Ground clearance	8.46in
Wading depth	19.7in
Max gradient	45°
Approach angle	39°
Departure angle	29° (without tow hitch)

NB Vehicle weights vary according to engine type and specification

the demise of the Classic, as well as in the all-conquering Defender range.

Initially only three-door versions of the Discovery were offered, and the V8 engine was carburettor-fed. But this changed after just nine months with the introduction of the more efficient injected V8 engine and the extremely welcome addition of two more doors. Combined, these two modifications transformed an already excellent machine into an even better one. A 2-litre petrol engine, the Rover Mpi, was also available from 1993, but this version is no longer offered. It provided many of the advantages of Discovery motoring but was seriously lacking in performance terms, and was unsuitable for off-road use or towing.

In the early days, many a hard-bitten Land Rover enthusiast dismissed the Discovery because of its body styling, despite the fact that, beneath the skin, the vehicle was every bit as tough as anything else from Solihull. Today, many of those same critics are themselves using and enjoying Discoverys, both for everyday use and for quite serious off-roading. Its styling, along with the reliable, efficient and frugal Tdi engine, has made the Discovery the most successful vehicle of its type, and one of the more commonly seen vehicles on British roads. Popular though the original Range Rover was, it could never have achieved the success of the Discovery.

In its latest form before the introduction of the re-vamped Discovery replacement range (scheduled for October 1998), the vehicle had been developed into an out-standing machine, offering high equipment levels, superb comfort, and an excellent performance/economy marriage with the 300 Tdi engine. Unlike the Defender, a V8 option was also available. The diesel version, available in 5-speed manual or 4-speed automatic, has proved the most popular. It has a top speed of 91mph

(146kph), and most owners are able to get around 30mpg on a run, whereas the 3.9-litre injected V8 – developed from the Buick 3.5 unit bought in by Rover in the mid-1960s – gives the Discovery 106mph (170kph) and about 21mpg.

With its high/low transfer box, long-travel coil suspension, and excellent ground clearance, the Discovery has all the versatility of the Defender, and off-roading abilities which are only restricted by its reduced approach and departure angles. It's a little more difficult to fit really big, grippy tyres for ultimate off-roading, yet in numerous Camel Trophy and other demanding events the vehicle has established off-roading credentials which are the envy of all its competitors. It is an irrefutable fact that none of the Discovery's rivals can even approach its rough-stuff performance. Despite all this,

Discovery owners enjoy excellent levels of refinement and comfort which are a very far cry from the earlier days of Land Rover ownership.

Range Rover

The original Range Rover was launched in 1970 and proved to be one of the most significant vehicles in the history of the British motor industry. Enthusiasts cried in their beer when it was announced that the Range Rover was to be replaced with an entirely new vehicle carrying the same name, and for a while the old version (by then dubbed the Classic) was produced alongside the new machine. When it was launched in September 1994 it was imme-diately apparent that the all-new Range Rover was, genuinely, all-new. Although the basic, estate-type body configuration

This is the diesel version of the Range Rover, the 2.5-litre BMW six-cylinder engine providing good road performance and excellent refinement. However, this version lacks low-down torque for towing or serious off-road work.

Range Rover specifications

Engine	2.5 litre 6-cylinder in-line turbo diesel indirect injection/4 litre V8 petrol injection/4.6 litre V8 petrol injection
Power	134bhp @ 4,400rpm/190bhp @ 4,750rpm/225bhp @ 4,750rpm
Torque	199lb/ft @ 2,300rpm/236lb/ft @ 3,000rpm/277lb/ft @ 3,000rpm
Transmission	5-speed manual/4-speed automatic permanent 4x4 with transfer box
Suspension	Live beam axles with electronic air suspension and variable ride height
Wheelbase	108in
Length	185.5in
Height (standard)	71.6in
Width	87.7in
Fuel capacity	20 gal (diesel)/22gal (petrol)
Towing weight (with over-run brakes)	3,500kg
Ground clearance	8.43in
Wading depth	19.7in (standard ride height)
Max gradient	45°
Approach angle	35° (maximum ride height)
Departure angle	26° (maximum ride height)

NB Vehicle weights vary according to engine type and specification

other than when seen from front three-quarters. The new machine was bigger, more spacious and with more luggage space than the Classic, and thoroughly modern in terms of its construction, equipment and use of electronics. While the original machine was showing its age in these respects – although not in its truly classic lines – the new Range Rover was, at the time of its launch, one of the world's most technologically advanced vehicles.

Although it followed in Land Rover traditions by having a separate chassis, this was of a completely new design, as were the front and rear suspension arrangements and the beam axles, the intention throughout having been to provide superb road-going performance, ride, and handling, along with the very best off-road characteristics. In addition there were three new engines. The long-lived V8 was fully redesigned in 4-litre and 4.6-litre versions, and there was also a BMW 2.5-litre straight six turbocharged diesel, used for the first time in a vehicle with off-road capability. The 4.6 has sports-car performance – 9.3secs 0–60mph (0–97kph) and a top speed of 125mph (201kph) – and the 4-litre is not a lot slower. The diesel gives respectable performance and good economy, although it lacks 'grunt' for heavy towing and serious off-roading. All three engine types are available in DT, SE, and HSE trim.

Levels of comfort and equipment are astonishing for a Solihull-built vehicle. The seats are the biggest and most luxurious ever used by Land Rover, while shoulder, head, and leg room are improved substantially all round when compared with its predecessor. One welcome development for rear seat passengers is that the rear wheel arches no longer protrude into the corners of the seats. The vehicle has variable ride height, developed from the automatic air suspension arrangement

of the original had been retained, there was little similarity between old and new, pioneered in the Range Rover LSE in 1992. The lowest (in normal use) of the five settings gives a ride 25mm (1in) below standard for improved stability and handling at high speed, while at 65mm (2.6in) below standard the Access setting aids vehicle entry and helps it squeeze beneath obstacles. At the other end of the scale, the higher settings are invaluable in some off-roading situations, giving extra clearance for front, rear, and sills, and lifting vulnerable parts further away from deep water and mud.

The Range Rover's advanced ABS system is the best around, and the only one suitable for off-road use. It collects data from each wheel, via its ECU, at an astonishing 250 times per second; when it senses a wheel is about to lock brake pressure is released and re-applied ten times a second. Related to the ABS system is the electronic traction control (which, like the advanced ABS, was pioneered on the original Range Rover), fitted as standard on HSE models, and available as an option on others. The system controls the distribution of torque across the rear axle at speeds of up to 30mph (48kph), and almost guarantees mobility in conditions which would otherwise bring the vehicle to a halt. The traction control unit uses the ability of the ABS to sense when a wheel is starting to spin and transfers torque to the wheel with the greatest grip. In extreme conditions, the centre differential is automatically locked through a viscous control unit whenever the system detects the slightest difference in adhesion between front and rear axles; together, the traction control and viscous locking centre differential are uncanny in their effectiveness.

All Range Rovers are available with either manual or automatic transmission. With the 5-speed manual, low range selection is made with an electronic button on the facia, but the 4-speed auto-matic has an H-gate selector which does not require a separate control for the transfer box – the first Land Rover vehicle to be thus equipped.

Freelander

Although it is quite radically different from any other Land Rover vehicle, there is still a noticeable family resemblance

Freelander specifications	
Engine	2-litre 4-cylinder in-line turbo diesel direct injection/1.8-litre 4-cylinder in-line petrol injection, both transverse mounted
Power	71.6kW @ 4,200rpm/88kW @ 5,550rpm
Torque	210Nm @ 2,000rpm/165Nm @ 2,750rpm
Transmission	5-speed manual with traction control
Suspension	Front, MacPherson struts, coil springs and anti-roll bar; rear, MacPherson strut trapezoidal link, coil springs
Wheelbase	100.6in
Length	172.6in
Height	69.5in
Width	71.4in
Fuel capacity	13 gal
Towing weight (with over-run brakes)	2,000kg
Ground clearance	7.6in
Approach angle	30°
Departure angle	34°

NB Vehicle weights vary according to engine type and specification

The Freelander is an excellent vehicle, especially with its 2-litre diesel engine. Performance and handling are superb, while road-holding is sports car-like. But don't expect traditional Land Rover off-roading capability.

about the Freelander, which is already taking the all-important leisure 4×4 market by storm. Available in three-door and five-door versions, along with a soft-top option, it is Land Rover's first chassis-less product, and the first to be designed with all-round use in mind, rather than having outright off-road performance as a principal consideration; but because much of its technology was developed in the Range Rover the Freelander is nevertheless reasonably competent when it is taken off the tarmac. It uses two engines developed initially for Rover cars, the K-series 1.8-litre petrol unit and the L-series 2-litre diesel, which has been further refined for use in the Freelander. Both are first-rate engines, and each gives exceptional road-going performance and fuel economy, while the diesel in particular provides acceptable off-road power characteristics.

There is no separate set of low gears as there is on all other Land Rovers; instead, full use has been made of the company's ABS technology and traction control expertise to provide a surprisingly effective alternative to the more conventional way of dealing with difficult off-road situations. Also tied in with the ABS system is the hill descent control, which provides safe off-road descending without the use of extra-low ratios and engine braking.

Revolutionary it might be – which is not the way Land Rover has developed new vehicles in the past – but there's no doubt that the Freelander is already the vehicle to beat in its market. And it probably marks the way forward for Land Rover in years to come.

Driving the family

World's best – by far

As you'd expect, the Defender is the most workmanlike of the range, in the level of trim, the driving position, and in the way it feels on the road. Yet the comfortable seats and levels of equipment are way beyond even the wildest dreams of Land Rover owners of the past. The 90 has the distinctive feel of any short wheelbase vehicle, with a slightly choppy ride and sometimes abrupt steering response – but, remember, the short wheelbase and minimal overhang at the front and rear contribute greatly to its unparalleled off-road ability. The 110 has better road manners than the 90, the extra wheelbase length improving the ride considerably, although when lightly laden even the 110 can feel a little jittery on any road with a less-than-smooth surface. All Land Rovers have a commanding driving position, offering an excellent view over the roofs of lesser vehicles and a great sense of being fully in control, but in the Defender this is at its best.

The 300 Tdi engine, which is by far the best diesel ever fitted to an off-road vehicle, complements the general characteristics of the Defender range to perfection. It's a ready starter, settling down immediately to the characteristic, although comparatively noisy beat of a direct injection diesel. On the road it powers the Defender along at quite respectable speeds, and even on fast-moving motorways it is never at a disadvantage, despite the unfavourable aerodynamics of the vehicle. But for all its ability on tarmac, it is on the rough stuff that the Defender comes into its own, and the diesel engine is most fully appreciated. Producing its maximum torque at only 1,800rpm ensures maximum control through all kinds of obstacle, and there's enough power available even on tick-over to enable the Defender to creep up difficult and steep terrain in first low with the driver fully in control. This amazing torque characteristic ensures immediate throttle response, and permits the use of relatively high gears when using the low

ratios, such as third or even fourth, to power through muddy situations which, if the driver was forced to use the lowest gears, would probably bring the vehicle to a standstill. The 110 doesn't have quite the off-road versatility of the 90 because of the way its greater rear overhang reduces the departure angle, and the slightly larger turning circle. Yet, because of the excellence of the Tdi engine, the vehicle is still better than anything available from other manufacturers.

Common to all Defenders and Discoverys is the superb, long-travel coil spring suspension pioneered in 1970 in the Range Rover, and introduced to the 'workhorse' Land Rovers when the 110 was launched in 1983, followed a year later by the 90. Operating in conjunction with live beam axles it provides extreme wheel articulation, maximising grip, and is responsible in no small way for the Defender's all-round ability.

Voyage of Discovery

Sharing, as it does, much of the working Land Rover's specification, the Discovery has a high proportion of the Defender's off-roading expertise, its only restrictions being reduced approach and departure angles, and limited wheel arch space which restricts tyre size without modification. Although more Discoverys are now being used by enthusiasts, and consequently being off-roaded more seriously, it remains a fact that most are used more or less exclusively as everyday cars. And although this role only utilises part of the Discovery's usefulness, it's an excellent way of getting around.

Based on the Range Rover Classic, and using the same chassis, the Discovery has a slightly softer, more relaxed ride than the vehicle it is derived from, which can seem a little 'nervous' on some surfaces. Along with this, the more modern interior

The versatility and toughness of the Discovery lends itself to arduous duties. This is one of three used as support vehicles for the BMW motorcycle team competing in the 1998 Paris–Dakar rally.

and lower levels of wind noise make the Discovery a particularly enjoyable vehicle to drive. With the diesel engine you get the advantages of economy, coupled with quite adequate performance, and levels of refinement which often surprise the first-timer. But for the ultimate in Discovery experiences try one with a V8 engine; the combination of silky power delivery and quietness transforms the car to a luxury limousine.

Least satisfactory of the engine options is the 2-litre Mpi (now found only on used vehicles). It is quite adequate for normal road use, although it lacks the torque of the diesel and the outright power of the V8, and because it has to work hard it consumes petrol at pretty

much the same rate as the 3.9. And it is not at all suitable for off-road use.

Rugged sophistication

The pinnacle of Land Rover engineering has always been the Range Rover, the latest version of which, launched in 1994, is a sensational machine in all respects. It has levels of comfort and sophistication which leave the opposition standing, yet, in the Solihull company's best traditions, possesses exceptional off-road capabilities. It's a large vehicle, yet the design is such that it doesn't feel at all intimidating when one sits behind the wheel. The driving position is superb, and there's more than enough room for another three adults and as much luggage as anyone could possibly want.

Top of the pile is the 4.6 V8 version, capable of whistling you along at 125mph (201kph) in total comfort and serenity – and if you can afford one, you're probably not going to be too bothered about the 17mpg fuel consumption figure which results from hard driving. The 4-litre V8 is a little less thirsty, nearly as fast, and just as smooth, probably making it the ideal compromise for many people. Taken from BMW car applications, the 2.5-litre turbocharged indirect injection diesel has proved a popular engine choice. It's so smooth and quiet that it can be mistaken for a petrol engine, even when ticking over, and has sufficient power for most owners, despite the size and weight of the vehicle. However, a heavy trailer or caravan hitched to the back of the Range Rover shows up the limitations of this otherwise excellent engine, and it simply doesn't have sufficient low-speed torque, bearing in mind the Range Rover's weight, for anything other than modest off-road operation. And yet it is off the beaten track that the Range Rover, when V8 powered, is at its most surprising, simply because you don't expect a vehicle this luxurious to be so good when dealing with axle-deep mud or rock-strewn mountain tracks.

The air suspension, with its variable ride height, means you can raise the body – although not, of course, the axles – to help cope with obstacles and deep water. At the very least, it reduces the risk of body damage, and improves the all-critical approach and departure angles. All Range Rovers have viscous centre differentials which lock automatically when the system senses a grip differential between front and rear axles, and the traction control system which is standard on the top-specification HSE can be specified as an extra

With the 4.6-litre V8 engine the Range Rover is fast, and capable of towing the heaviest trailer or caravan. Fuel consumption, however, can be as poor as 16–17mpg.

on other models. It's a remarkable device, giving the Range Rover more effective grip than any other Land Rover vehicle.

The ABS system, which also acts as part of the traction control arrangement, is unique in that it provides effective and safe braking in extreme off-road conditions. With other vehicles, engine braking is the only option for steep, dangerous descents off-road, but with the Range Rover you can use the brakes with complete confidence.

Land Rover Junior

The baby of the Land Rover family, the Freelander, is more of a road-going compromise than the Discovery, and is poised to make very significant inroads into the hitherto Japanese-dominated recreational vehicle market. It's an excellent vehicle; it can be thrown around like a sports car, it has the comfort levels of the best medium-size saloons, yet it still has reasonable off-road ability. It is the first Land Rover to be built as a monocoque, without a separate chassis, and the first not to have a transfer box for extra-low gear ratios. And yet, despite its non-traditional design approach, the Freelander boasts an off-road performance which, although not a match for its excellent road-going attributes, is ahead of the game when compared with its rivals.

As with the Range Rover, full use is made of Land Rover's advanced ABS system to provide an electronic control system which maintains traction in the most difficult of situations. As with the Range Rover, the system shifts torque to whichever wheel on an axle is gripping, and, through its viscous transmission coupling, effectively ensures there is grip at both axles. It overcomes, to a degree, the absence of the more conventional low-ratios in descent situations with its unique hill descent control, which automatically applies the brakes in difficult descents to maintain a steady descent speed of 5.6mph (9kph). It even senses when the route is twisting and/or undulating, when it reduces the speed even more. However, its performance off the tarmac cannot be compared with that of other Land Rover vehicles, despite what has been said by some commentators, understandably so much in love with the vehicle that they have run away with themselves when it comes to assessing the Freelander as an off-roader.

There are two principal problems. Firstly, the absence of separate low ratios through a transfer box means that even the truly excellent diesel engine cannot cope with difficult obstacles requiring very slow speeds. The only way to attempt to overcome this in the Freelander, when difficulties such as ditches, gullies, and rock steps require very slow speed, is to attempt to control the vehicle speed with the clutch, trying to keep forward speed down to perhaps one or two miles an hour and at the same time endeavouring to keep the engine at its optimum torque point for best response. Inevitably, this results too often in stalls at the most critical moments, and the vehicle fails to overcome the obstacle. It doesn't take much of this for the clutch to start burning (not surprisingly), with the consequent risk of losing it altogether, and certainly shortening its life expectancy. There are also problems with difficult downhill situations. A Defender or Discovery descending a steep hill in first low under engine braking is doing no more than 2mph (3.2kph), and is fully under control. But a Freelander's hill descent control limits the speed to 5.6mph (9kph) most of the time, or sometimes a little less through the braking system, and this is twice as fast as you want to be going in many situations.

The other main worries with the Freelander when off-roading are the lack of wheel movement — which when compared with Land Rover's other vehicles is seriously restricted — and the lack of ground clearance. The traction control system and the viscous coupling providing front/rear axle slip control can only work effectively when wheels have at least some contact with the ground, and lack of wheel articulation inhibits the potential of the system. Ground clearance, too, is inadequate for anything other than occasional off-roading.

On the face of it, it is difficult to choose between the two engine choices. The same 1.8-litre 16 valve petrol engine used in the MGF sports car is one option, while the L-series 2-litre direct injection turbo diesel is the other. Both are excellent units, although anyone planning to use a Freelander for towing, or the modest off-roading of which it is capable, would probably prefer the diesel, which offers quite outstanding on-road performance, superb economy (40mpg is easily achievable) and yet at the same time has extremely useful low-speed torque characteristics.

It may not be in the same league as other Land Rover machinery when it comes to off-roading, but the Freelander is an excellent vehicle. It was not designed to go rock climbing or mud plugging, but as an excellent 'lifestyle' vehicle with superb road manners, very good performance, excellent levels of comfort, and acceptable off-road ability — and is yet another in a very long line of superb products from Solihull.

It is, without doubt, another winner.

Chapter Two

A legend is born

Despite the romantic appeal of the story, the Land Rover was not created simply as a replacement for the wartime Jeep. It's a popular legend with a nice ring to it, but there's a lot more to the birth of the legend than that. A number of unrelated circumstances were to lead, in a roundabout way, to the Rover company coming up with the first generation of a vehicle destined to transform the lives of outdoor workers around the world and to form the nucleus of one of the great success stories of motor manufacturing.

It is difficult to imagine a world without Land Rovers, particularly for anyone

This is the most famous Land Rover of them all, HUE 166, the first production vehicle of 1948. Many enthusiasts believe that the shape was at its purest with the original 80-inch wheelbase.

involved in agriculture, forestry, upland management, road construction, the African and Australian bush, and a thousand other situations which require all-terrain mobility regardless of climate and conditions. In one sense, the story of the Land Rover can be said to have begun when the American Government had the foresight to invite designs for a compact, highly mobile, general-purpose vehicle when it was suddenly plunged into the Second World War. Willys and Ford were destined to build a great many of the GPs (Jeeps) which resulted, and they became a common sight around Britain as the war raged on. When hostilities ended, a considerable number ended up in civilian hands, and among the many people who were able to appreciate the advantages of everyday four-wheel drive transportation was Maurice Wilks, chief

engineer of Rover, who acquired one for use on his 250-acre Welsh estate.

In those immediate post-war days, life was very, very hard, and in some ways worse than it had been during the war, with especially harsh rationing, major shortages of all kinds, and very little private transport. Rover, like other car makers, was severely hampered in its efforts to get back into car production by the acute shortage of steel, the Government, when it came to releasing steel for manufacture, favouring those companies with export programmes from which desperately needed foreign currency would be derived. In addition Rover had a massive factory at Solihull – built for wartime aircraft and tank engine manufacture – for which it simply did not have production capacity. The company could not present an export programme because

This is how the Land Rover might have been. This 1947 prototype had centre steering and curved wings, both of which were dropped because of production difficulties and expense. There is considerable similarity to the Willys Jeep at this very early stage of Land Rover development. (National Motor Museum)

it only had pre-war models to offer; in terms of future planning, the company had gone to sleep while involved in wartime manufacturing.

Maurice Wilks and his brother Spencer came up, initially, with the idea of building a utilitarian car, matching the mood of the times, which would use as little sheet steel as possible. But although there was time enough to call it the M (for miniature) 1, the project never really got off the ground, principally because it was thought there wouldn't really be a market for it. Then Maurice suggested building a vehicle like the Jeep, for which there was no replacement, as a stop-gap exercise until steel restrictions were eased. It would, the brothers stated, bring in much-needed cash for Rover, would utilise some of the idle production capacity, and, if built largely of aluminium (which was in relatively plentiful supply)

would circumvent much of the raw material shortage problem.

In the spring of 1947 it was decided to proceed, although there was considerable misgiving within Rover at the prospect of coming up with a light utility four-wheel drive vehicle, which could not have been more different from the traditional and somewhat staid cars people at Rover were accustomed to. Maurice christened the vehicle the Land Rover when it was still only at the idea stage – simple, yes, but what inspiration!

Although he was to maintain firm control, Maurice put Robert Boyle in charge of design. There was to be no expensive tooling for the Land Rover, simply because it was never intended to be around for long enough to pay back the costs. So instead of expensive presses for chassis members, strips of steel were simply welded into box sections which

Here is another photograph of HUE 166, the first production Land Rover, standing alongside a very early Series IIA 88-inch in 1969. (National Motor Museum)

were then formed into complete chassis assemblies. The original idea of having centre steering, overcoming production problems associated with right-hand and left-hand drive, was dropped because it was not practical in use. Pleasantly curved front wings had initially been part of the plan too, but this element of the design was abandoned in favour of box-like bodywork, which was much simpler, and cheaper, to manufacture. Thus was born one of the most distinctive visual characteristics of the Land Rover, and one which lives on to this day in the Defender.

As many standard Rover parts as possible were used, including a slightly adapted version of the 1,595cc inlet-over-exhaust engine developed for the P3 saloon, due for launch in 1948. The prototype engine had been a pre-war 1,389cc Rover Ten unit, which was desperately short of power for the new application. The basic gearbox

also came from the P3, but with a very useful step-down ratio. A quite sophisticated permanent four-wheel drive transmission was developed, with a free-wheel device between the transfer box and the front prop shaft, a much better system than the one used in the Jeep. In fact, although the Jeep had inspired the Land Rover, the Solihull vehicle was very different, and much more useful. So much so, that Rover was quite taken aback with the general reaction to the new baby after its unveiling at the 1948 Amsterdam Motor Show. It received an ecstatic welcome from the press, and farmers started clamouring for them, as did people in less developed countries, who, suddenly, had the opportunity to buy a vehicle capable of coping with unmade roads, or no roads at all. Within no time production of the Land Rover had exceeded the company's car output.

Despite the success there was no sitting

One of the very rare 80-inch station wagons on Land Rover's factory display at the 1998 Billing Show. The vehicle was produced in 1949.

back, and development continued. The free-wheel was discontinued in 1950 and in came a dog clutch arrangement which ensured the full-time availability of engine braking on all four wheels. Also introduced was a system enabling the selection of two-wheel drive in the high gears, although all four wheels were engaged in low ratios. In the second half of 1951 came another welcome development, an increase in engine size to 1,997cc, overcoming the most commonly-heard complaint – lack of power. As it happened, the engine produced only marginally more power, but a lot more torque; as it was torque which mattered, especially when

These are the sort of conditions which helped endear Land Rovers to generations of farmers. The photograph shows the author enjoying the Series IIA which he ran for many years.

towing, carrying heavy loads, and using the power take-off facility, the change of engine was to prove highly significant. In fact, this engine was not destined to last for long. In late-1953 the vehicle was given a new spread-bore 2-litre engine, with water channels between all the cylinders, at the same time as the original 80-inch wheelbase was replaced with the more versatile 86-inch version, and a completely new long wheelbase version, the 107-inch was introduced, initially available only as a pick-up.

By now, the Land Rover had firmly established itself as a tough, go-anywhere vehicle. It was liked greatly by farmers and industrialists, and was being put to good use in the burgeoning post-war construction industry. It was popular as a pint-sized fire engine, capable of being driven around factories and into narrow alleyways out of bounds to conventional machinery, and was catching on as a breakdown vehicle, among uncountable other workhorse applications.

Wheelbases were stretched again in 1956, to 88 inches and 109 inches, a configuration destined to survive for many years. There were many raised eyebrows when it was realised that the extra two inches had been used between the front axle and bulkhead and not the all-important load area. Then in June 1957 the wheelbase mystery was solved when Land Rover announced a new engine, the long-awaited diesel ... which was impossible to fit into the earlier engine bay, hence the extra couple of inches. The 2,052cc diesel, with wet liners and overhead valves with roller tappets, was designed to have a speed range very close to the current petrol engines, thereby enabling the same transmission to be used, and permitting the interchangeability of units. Unfortunately it could not be retro-fitted into the 86-inch and 107-inch vehicles.

More than 200,000 Land Rovers were

Land Rovers were working machines long before they gained a recreational use. Here a 1960 Series II is being used as a mobile workshop for emergency repairs to a plough. (National Motor Museum)

manufactured in the first ten years – twice the number of Rover cars – and there's no doubt about the impact of the utility vehicle on Rover's fortunes. A further major boost to Land Rover production came when the British Army announced in 1956 that the Land Rover was to become its standard lightweight four-wheel drive vehicle; but even without this there was no doubt at all that the hard-working machine conceived by Maurice Wilks was already Britain's outstanding motoring success story.

Second generation

The original Land Rovers, retrospectively known as the Series I, gave way to the Series II in 1958, although the act of succession was not what might be called a slick affair. The 107-inch continued for a while, with the 2-litre petrol engine, while only the 109-inch could be obtained with the new and better 2,286cc unit. This was a re-worked version of the old petrol engine, now without cylinder liners, and with a much improved head. Power output was up by 25 per cent. However, important as this was, David Bache's styling department had taken a long, hard look at the Land Rover. The result was a more rounded body, with 1.5in (38mm) added to the width, in turn permitting the use of a wider track and better turning circle, and skirts around the sides hiding the exhaust and chassis. The bonnet had a little more shape, too. You could even choose from a full range of colours. The Series II launch was completed with the introduction of the 109-

This Series II 109-inch diesel is being used to tow and power one of the mobile X-ray clinics that were part of everyday life in 1959, when this photograph was taken. Electricity for the X-ray equipment came from a large alternator which was powered by the Land Rover's power take-off shaft. (National Motor Museum)

inch Station Wagon – a considerable improvement over the earlier 107-inch – in the autumn of 1958.

Although the Series II was only in production for three years, it was an eventful period in the history of the marque, with success piling on success, and the Australian and Swiss armies following the lead of the British in choosing the Land Rover for military use. Production passed the quarter-million mark in November 1959. The Series II gave way to the much-loved IIA in the autumn of 1961, although the new designation was prompted more by a change in the company's chassis number system than in major alterations to the vehicle. Indeed, not a great deal happened to the vehicles from the end of Series II production to the introduction of the Series III in 1971.

There was one highly significant event, however, which would endear the Land Rover to its customers even more, and further enhance its already vast respect as

a working machine. This was the new diesel engine. The old 2-litre diesel, by now a well-established option, was somewhat puny, and quickly got out of its depth when towing heavy loads, particularly in parts of the world where the terrain was anything other than Fenland flat. The new engine had been under development for some time, and shared the same dimensions as the petrol unit. Combustion chamber design permitted the continuation of a three main bearing crank, as in the petrol unit, and the additional 16lb/ft of torque greatly enhanced the appeal of Land Rover's diesel.

Last of the 'leafers'

The Series III came along in 1971, but by then a number of important things had

RIGHT Land Rovers have been utilised by both of Britain's major automobile clubs, as demonstrated by this 1972 vehicle in RAC colours. (Phil Talbot)

happened which affected, one way or another, the world-wide 4×4 market. Most importantly, by June 1970 Rover had successfully developed and introduced an entirely new type of four-wheel drive vehicle. The Range Rover pioneered the use by Land Rover of the ex-Buick 3.5-litre V8 engine, which was also used in the Rover P5 and then the P6 saloon. It was also Land Rover's first vehicle to use low-rate coil springs, giving undreamed-of ride comfort, and the first time it had been deemed necessary to provide creature comforts for driver and passengers.

Research in 1966 had indicated that, while Land Rovers dominated the 4×4 market, two-thirds of Land Rovers were being used for recreational purposes or for general transport rather than agricultural use. While the recreational aspect may have had validity in North America, where Land Rover were doing quite well despite home-grown 4×4s by Jeep, Ford, and others, common sense and general observation were sufficient to prove that the vast majority were being used by farmers and others connected with the land. The Land Rover enthusiast movement, which would change things so much in the 1980s, had yet to become significant.

A third development had been the use, for the first time, of a powerful engine in a Land Rover, when a V6 version of the Buick V8 was played around with in 1965. In the event, with work on the 'Roverisation' of the V8 progressing well

Among the many different types of Land Rovers, fire engines are popular with today's enthusiasts. This 1971 fire engine is owned by Vic Barrington-Wise of Northampton.

in connection with the P5 saloon and then the embryonic Range Rover project, the idea of a V6 was abandoned. In its place a special version of the 2,625cc P4 car engine was developed for Land Rover use, being installed first in the hitherto under-powered Forward Control, whose vast weight and bulk required more grunt than the 2.25-litre petrol engine could provide.

A beefed-up version of the engine was offered initially to the North American market in the 109-inch Station Wagon, but it was not successful off-road because it had to be taken to 3,000rpm to obtain maximum torque, and the US option only lasted a year. However, it was destined to remain an option for the British 109-inch IIA, and then the Series III until the V8 was offered in 1980. It was prodigiously thirsty, though, and nowhere near as suit-able as the V8 proved itself in the Range Rover and then the Series III. Perhaps the most interesting point of all this is that it showed the company was aware that there was a power deficiency problem with the standard engines, although the six-cylinder was never a serious answer, as those owners who opted for them discovered.

As had been the case with the Series IIA, the Series III was not greatly different to the model it replaced in September 1971, but the improvements it did have were significant and long overdue. The new grille layout made the new model easy to identify, while the revised facia design and instrument layout at last dragged the cabin out of the 1950s. The one technical development which was much appreciated, and which added greatly to the ease of driving the new vehicle heavily laden or towing weighty trailers, was the gearbox modification which gave owners synchromesh on first and second gears. In conjunction with this the 9.5-inch heavy duty clutch was stan-dardised, along with reduced clutch pedal pressure, stronger half-shafts on the long

wheelbase versions, better brakes, and an improved electrical system.

Three years later, in the summer of 1974, came something which Land Rover owners had long required – an overdrive. It took the 1973 oil crisis to force the issue, but Tom Barton's request for ten-ders from established accessory companies led to the now-familiar Fairey two-speed auxiliary gearbox which so transforms a leaf-sprung Land Rover's main road cruis-ing and fuel consumption. Fortunately, the design was such that it could be fitted to any Series II, IIA or III Land Rover in just a few hours; hundreds of thousands of owners around the world have since wel-comed the Fairey unit with its 28 per cent overdrive gearing.

First utility V8

There had still been no satisfactory answer for those owners who wanted more power than the standard engines could provide and for whom the six-cylinder option wasn't satisfactory. But under the Ryder reorganisation plan of the late-1970s, which affected the entire British Leyland conglomerate, Land Rover was established as an independent company in 1978 and took over the Solihull factory. More significantly, a massive investment programme was announced for the com-pany. An important part of this was the decision to introduce a new Land Rover model with the V8 engine, by now well proven in the enormously successful Range Rover and the 101-inch Forward Control.

The V8 had initially found its way into Land Rovers during mid-1960s develop-ment work on the engine when a batch of 88-inch vehicles had been used as mobile test beds; more recently, and not at all surprisingly, official development work had been going the same way. Not only that, but numerous owners, tired of wait-

The most important model of recent years has been the Discovery. This three-door model was one of Land Rover's stars at the 1990 Frankfurt Motor Show. (National Motor Museum)

ing for Land Rover to do the right thing, had fitted their own.

The Series III V8, known as the Stage 1 because it was the first stage in the development of an all-new utility Land Rover, was first available in the early spring of 1979; the 3,528cc unit was detuned from its Range Rover specification (which, in turn, was less powerful than the car version) and produced 91bhp and, more importantly, 15,66lb/ft of torque. At last there was a speedy Land Rover, which could do 80mph (129kph), while the torque transformed its towing ability and further enhanced it as an off-roader. Unfortunately, however, it was only available with the 109-inch versions, and there were many 88-inch owners envious of the extra power and smoothness, and the permanent four-wheel drive and lockable centre differential which had, of course, also been transplanted into the working

machine. A completely new vehicle, which would be introduced as the One Ten, was planned for the early 1980s, but in the meantime the existing petrol and diesel four-cylinder engines were re-engineered in 1980 and, among other improvements, given five-bearing cranks. The 2.5-litre diesel, to be introduced later, would benefit greatly from that particular innovation.

Although the coil sprung One Ten was launched in 1983, followed a year later by the Ninety, the Series III remained in production until 1985, partly for overseas customers and partly to satisfy back orders which buyers did not want to change. The last Series III to be built, a left-hand drive 109-inch Station Wagon, was preserved for the Heritage Motor Museum after leaving the production line at the end of 1985 – the end of a fine family which had begun life 37 years earlier.

Chapter Three

Land Rovers
at play

The Land Rover enthusiast movement is stronger than any of those connected with other marques. Even in the classic car world, where Jaguar, Morris Minor and MG tower above all else, nothing begins to approach the passion which flows from those who love Land Rovers. There is, of course, a major difference between the classic car movement and the world of Land Rovers. A large proportion

There has been a powerful, Land Rover-based, off-road competition scene for a very long time. In this photograph, celebrated Land Rover artist and cartoonist Pete Wilford negotiates a very tight section in his Series I trialler at Eastnor Castle in 1971.

of classic car owners shine up their vehicles for weekend shows and rallies, but restrict driving to just a couple of thousand miles a year, and never in the rain if it can be avoided. Land Rovers, though, were built to work – and work they do, no matter how old, whether or not they've been restored. Land Rover owners do enjoy lining up their vehicles to be admired by others, but show most drivers a stretch of rough ground or a sea of mud and they'll head straight for it.

There are countless clubs, innumerable events, and a huge industry supplying everything from complete vehicles to engine pushrods, and army surplus fuel drums to expensive accessories for Range Rovers. Just one of the annual events, the *Land Rover Owner International* show and rally held at Billing, Northampton, every July, eclipses all other motoring events – save, perhaps the British Grand Prix – for the rampant enthusiasm it generates. And

the magazine which puts on this annual feast, *Land Rover Owner International* (invariably shortened to *Land Rover Owner*), is one of the biggest and most influential of all motoring publications.

The Land Rover enthusiast movement began quietly in the 1950s and at first grew slowly, before exploding in the mid-1980s to become the massive phenomenon it is now. When working with IPC in 1984, I launched Britain's first glossy four-wheel drive magazine, *4 Wheel Drive*, and it struggled for copy sales because, as the marketing people put it, 'it was ahead of its market'. Coincidentally, at the very same time David Bower, who these days runs a thriving off-road business in a delightful corner of Devon, was in the process of turning his established and popular *Overlander* newsletter-type publication into a glossy magazine in conjunction with Link House. His magazine, like mine, found it hard going at first, but Link

Land Rovers are able to take you right away from it all. These three vehicles are enjoying an off-roading outing in the mountains of central Wales.

House stuck with it more than IPC, and eventually the two merged to become *Off-Road and 4 Wheel Drive*.

Yet only three years after those enjoyable times back in 1984, another new magazine came on the scene. Unlike the others, this was exclusively Land Rover orientated, and initially it was targeted at the 'hunting, shooting and fishing' types, because its publishers believed the up-market set who were then using Range Rovers and Land Rover County Station Wagons were interested in buying a magazine about their vehicles. The magazine was called *Land Rover Owner*, and it had come along just as the enthusiast movement was shifting from second into third gear. It changed its emphasis after a short while, and began reflecting the activities and vehicles of keen Land Rover people, since when it has never looked back; years of hard work by the three men behind it – Richard Green, John Cornwall (who had the original idea), and Richard Thomas – led to its development into a major force in motoring publishing while, simultaneously, the Land Rover enthusiast movement grew into what we know today.

There had, of course, been Land Rover enthusiasts practically from the very beginning, and there was certainly a passionate, if not terribly large, enthusiast movement by the time the Series II was launched in 1958. My own enthusiasm was typical, and was sparked off in the mid-1960s by a farmer friend who went with me in his Series II to a motorcycle trial in Wales in which I was competing; he worked his Land Rover around his fields, but also played with it, and it was he who demonstrated to me the impressive off-road abilities of the machine.

Clubs and competitors

Over the years more and more clubs began to spring up, off-roading competi-

One of Britain's most respected restorers of early Land Rovers is Ken Wheelwright, here being interviewed about his contribution to the classic Land Rover scene by journalist and off-road expert David Bowyer.

tions (at the time consisting almost exclusively of the popular sport of trialling) became dominated by Land Rovers, with the particularly compact dimensions of Series Is making them especially popular with participants. It was not long after the introduction of the Range Rover in 1970 that it was realised that a Series I into which a Range Rover V8 had been grafted was practically unbeatable, other than by another similarly modified machine. This led, initially, to domination of the sport by the few people far-sighted enough to invest in V8 engines and the far from straightforward conversion of their Series

Is. Then, spurred on by the success of the few, a lot more people looked firstly at the Series I and secondly at the V8. The advantages of the Range Rover coil spring suspension were also quickly appreciated by triallists.

But there was also growth in a general, non-sporting enthusiasm for Land Rovers, which had commenced in a fairly small way in the early 1960s, and then slowly, but relentlessly, gathered momentum. By the late-1970s there were enough enthusiasts around for the Land Rover movement to start becoming a noticeable force and, as with all enthusiast-based activities, the club scene was to prove important.

In some ways there were parallels with the classic car movement, which grew rapidly during the 1970s, but unlike the car scene, a Land Rover didn't have to be historic for a club to be formed for its followers. In 1987 I was a member of the Range Rover Register, when the vehicle was a mere 17 years old, and yet my membership number was 475. The chairman was then Dave Mitchell, who had been in on the start of the club (formed by Bill King in 1984–5), whose off-road training facilities in Bala, North Wales, are among the best in Britain and who, at the last count, was a member of 14 clubs connected with Land Rovers, and on the committees of four. And yes, Dave, like me, is still nuts about Range Rovers.

These days there are clubs catering specifically for all types of Land Rover, with, at the time of writing, more than a dozen organisations operating on a national basis, and an amazing total of just over 100 regional clubs, each one of them exclusively Land Rover. While some of the clubs, notably the two organisations for Series I machines, the Series II and Series III clubs, and the Range Rover Register, cater enthusiastically and knowledgeably for classic vehicles, many of them are also involved in off-roading

activities. These range from extremely demanding trials for specially-built and modified machines, to non-damaging events for normal road-going vehicles, with safari runs for those who just want to enjoy a gentle saunter over easy terrain in the company of like-minded people.

The competition scene

The most difficult, and most specialist, side of the off-roading scene is for the heavily modified machines competing in the CCV (cross country vehicle) classes, in which there are various categories. Competition is fierce and the going really does get tough, yet the camaraderie of the sport is an object lesson to most other forms of motorsport. More and more clubs are organising events at this extreme end of the spectrum, with club, regional, and national championships ensuring a continuously lively – to say the least – level of activity. The machinery involved ranges from fairly standard-looking, but enormously potent Series Is, through Range Rovers, to vehicles which would seem to have more right to be roaming around Mars. Increasingly popular are heavily modified Range Rovers with very shortened rear ends ('bob tails'). Less arduous, and certainly less demanding on the pocket, are the events for RTVs (road-taxed vehicles), but even here the competition can be such that you have to be exceptionally competent to win. And the growing level of competition means that vehicles are steadily becoming more specialised, despite having to be road legal.

Most people catch the off-roading bug after enjoying a safari run around an off-roading area, possibly while competitive events are underway. There's usually such a buzz in the atmosphere, along with the compelling smell of mud drying on hot exhaust pipes, that newcomers are unable

Not all off-road activities are as hard as this, where a Defender is being assisted manually over a log 'trap' during selection trials for the Camel Trophy. (Nick Dimbleby)

to resist getting caught up in it all. At one time the way into off-roading for many enthusiasts was to go greenlaning, enjoying a run along tracks classified as public byways but normally only used by farmers, walkers, and horse-riders. However, the whole business of greenlaning has become something of a political hot potato, and a growing number of greenlanes are becoming reclassified by county councils to cut out recreational driving. But there are still enough greenlanes to go round, and there's probably no better way to enjoy the off-roading capabilities of a Land Rover than a gentle drive along tracks which are impassable to normal cars. Some of the most popular, and certainly the most challenging, are in mid-Wales, where it is still possible to go on a

truly adventurous expedition into the mountains and, especially in bad weather, experience really tough conditions for which drivers need to be experienced and vehicles well equipped. Unfortunately, over-use and irresponsible behaviour by some sectors of the off-roading movement have led to clashes with local farmers and the loss of some of the routes.

A few rules *must* be observed whenever a greenlaning outing is being considered. Make certain that vehicular traffic is permitted (this may mean checking it out with the county council); never travel alone, but in company with one or two other vehicles, in case of difficulty; take basic recovery equipment with you (winch or tow rope, high-lift jacks, etc); drive slowly; avoid causing damage; leave all gates as you found them; respect farm animals and wildlife; and show courtesy to other users.

The Billing jamboree

Of course, not everyone with a Land Rover is interested in getting covered with mud at every opportunity. There's a thriving restoration scene for older vehicles, and many clubs have concours (or similar) competitions at their local and national rallies. And, of course, despite the strength of the club movement a large number of Land Rover enthusiasts choose not to become members of clubs, preferring instead to enjoy their vehicles on their own or with a small group of friends. This is, perhaps, at its most evident every July, when Land Rover people from all over the world descend on Billing Aquadrome, Northampton, for the annual jamboree organised by *Land Rover Owner* magazine.

There is nothing else like Billing, as the event is known, anywhere in the world. The massive area of the Aquadrome, which can play host to perhaps half-a-dozen normal events simultaneously, as well as its regular weekend influx of holidaymakers, is taken over totally by this one celebration. It becomes a sea of Land Rovers of every type, from the earliest Series Is to the latest Range Rovers and Freelanders, along with countless thousands of enthusiasts and an entire shopping centre of trade stands. More than 1,500 caravans and the biggest array of tents to be seen anywhere fill every corner of the huge riverside complex.

The event was the brainchild of two of the key people behind the present-day enthusiast movement, Richard Green and John Cornwall, who have seen it grow from simply a small gathering of enthusiasts in just one of Billing's event fields, to a jumbo-sized celebration of the marque;

There is even an enthusiast movement among young children. This perfectly scaled miniature Series I completes a battery-powered tour of the arena at the 1997 Billing Show.

Among the more bizarre ways of enjoying Land Rovers is to race them, despite their well-deserved reputation for lack of pace. Here a stripped-down Series I is being campaigned with vigour at Silverstone in 1954. (National Motor Museum)

Richard and John are still the central figures in the show's organisation. Visitors come from every part of the world, with groups and individuals travelling specially from Japan, the USA, Australia, and New Zealand, as well as hundreds who drive their treasured Land Rovers from Europe and Scandinavia.

The heart of the event, which has become virtually a week-long affair, is the non-stop programme of activities in the central arena under the masterful hand of Dave Bowyer. Older machinery is celebrated with line-ups from the various clubs representing Series I, Series II and IIA, and Series III vehicles, with Range Rovers, Discoverys, modern Land Rovers, and military enthusiasts also very much in evidence. The concours-type line-ups rep-

resent the very best collection of restored, renovated, and generally cherished Land Rover vehicles to be found anywhere. All this is fully complemented by displays of winching and general recovery techniques, driving demonstrations, and fun-packed sessions in which enthusiasts can show their own skills.

The Billing event provides living proof of the amazing strength and depth of Land Rover enthusiasm. Those who visit out of curiosity come away as enthusiasts, while everyone else simply gets more committed every year. Richard Green is extremely optimistic about the show's future. 'As far as I am concerned we will be staging it at Billing until at least 2002,' he told me, 'which is as far ahead as it is possible to look. Essentially, the only problem we have to face each year is the fact that it just keeps getting bigger, but we haven't yet fully outgrown the location.'

The Land Rover press

There are three central pivots to the Land Rover movement: the vehicles themselves, the clubs, and the 'big boy' of the specialist press, *Land Rover Owner* magazine. Each issue of *LRO* (as it is known to enthusiasts throughout the world) contains an excellent mix of articles on every aspect of every type of Land Rover. Enthusiasts write about their expeditions to the deserts, mountains, and jungles of the world, and there are in-depth stories about people and their vehicles. Servicing, repairs, maintenance, and renovation are fully covered, reflecting the very do-it-yourself nature of Land Rover ownership, and you can learn everything from rebuilding an early gearbox to mechanical improvements for machinery as up-to-date and sophisticated as the most recent Defenders and Range Rovers.

The magazine's editor, Carl Rodgerson is a dedicated enthusiast and skilled professional journalist, and promises that *LRO* will always serve up the most appetising menus enthusiasts could wish for. 'Nobody is more aware than I that *LRO* is part of the movement,' he told me, 'not some detached onlooker in the way of some motoring publications. Because those

Some people are so enthusiastic about their Land Rovers that they use them every day and take them to shows at weekends. Professional photographer Chris Bentley uses his 1964 Series IIA for work, yet somehow manages to keep it immaculate.

of us running the magazine are so much in touch with enthusiasts around the world, we know what people want and try desperately to give it.' He believes that the enthusiast movement will continue to develop as more inexpensive Range Rovers become available, and as the cost of Discoverys falls more within the reach of everyday people. 'The large number of Discoverys in circulation ensures the growing use of them by enthusiasts, who are able to combine everyday, family use with all the things Land Rover people want to do with their vehicles. Indeed, the Discovery is crucial to the future of the enthusiast movement.' Crucially, *LRO* – which is packed with advertising relating to the enjoyment and maintenance of Land Rovers – contains full listings of clubs and their membership contacts, along with a rolling programme of forthcoming events. Each month, the magazine reports on a representative assortment of club activities.

The massive growth of the Land Rover enthusiast movement has led to the development of a huge industry specialising in the manufacture and supply of parts, conversion companies, vehicle sales specialists, renovation and restoration organisations, engine and gearbox specialists, and companies selling genuine Land Rover parts right back to Series I. And, of course, there's the network of franchised Land Rover dealers for the supply of new and recent vehicles, parts, and servicing. With all this reflected in the magazine, each issue is effectively a *Yellow Pages* of the world of Land Rovers.

Another major sector of the movement, and one which has grown enormously over recent years, is in off-road tuition, and a check through *Land Rover Owner* reveals numerous specialists offering everything from basic off-road driving lessons to advanced techniques suitable for expeditions anywhere in the world, and,

of course, the most advanced recovery and survival information. Some of these organisations have acquired world-wide recognition, yet each one will provide one-to-one tuition which, after a day of mixed 'classroom', driving, and demonstration, will prepare even the most inexperienced of drivers for relatively advanced off-roading situations. Off-roading can be dangerous, and tuition of this type cannot be recommended too highly.

Another service offered by these companies is the opportunity to follow-up basic instruction with as much first-hand experience on their off-road centres as you feel you need. Having somewhere to practise and develop driving and recovery techniques is invaluable; not only does it build confidence, but it also minimises the risk of damage to valuable vehicles.

Two other publications specific to the marque are *Land Rover World* and *Land Rover Monthly*. The first covers the broad Land Rover enthusiast scene in a very informal way. It caters for all types of Land Rover owners, but concentrates to some extent on those with older and less expensive vehicles. Each issue carries a selection of technical and practical articles. *Land Rover Monthly* is new to the scene and only the first issue had been seen at the time of writing. It is believed that this publication will concentrate its coverage on the various aspects of off-roading, including competition at all levels, thereby distancing itself from the broad-brush approach of *Land Rover Owner* and *Land Rover World*.

Land Rovers in miniature

There's a massive interest in model Land Rovers, with enthusiasts all over the world eager to buy models, either reflecting an interest in just one particular vehicle or, at the other extreme, building collections which can run into several

Dave Mitchell somehow finds time to be the world's largest retailer of model Land Rovers, despite also running a thriving off-road school at Bala, North Wales, and being involved in the organisation of major events.

There is massive interest in collecting model Land Rovers, which is not at all surprising when they are as good as this.

One of the most enthusiastically supported of all Land Rover models is the Lightweight, or Air Portable. Here a group from the Lightweight Club gather for a display at a show.

hundred vehicles. The world's largest retailer of model Land Rovers is Dave Mitchell, who combines his model business with his Landcraft off-roading activities in Bala, North Wales. Like so many things, this successful operation came about more or less by chance, and started because of Dave's interest in buying the occasional model Land Rover to match up with full-size vehicles he had owned. The current stock list runs to around 500 different miniature Land Rovers, although the total list over the years extends to more than a thousand. Dave's models are sourced from suppliers throughout the world, although the principal manufacturing country by far, these days, is China.

Since he began selling models, Dave has found that the Series I Land Rover has always been the best seller, followed by the Lightweight, and this remains the case

today, despite the fact that his stock of models includes all the latest Land Rover vehicles and is right up to date with a delightful Freelander with working doors, steering, and suspension. The most expensive model currently stocked by Dave costs about £550, and the fact that people are quite happy to pay hundreds of pounds for a model Land Rover reflects the degree of enthusiasm there is for the marque generally. And few are more enthusiastic than Dave – his own collection of tiny Land Rovers is one of the largest, and most valuable, in the world.

Land Rovers in print and video

Richard Green, one of the co-founders of *Land Rover Owner* magazine, is the largest supplier anywhere of books, videos, and general Land Rover memorabilia. Founded as a parallel business to the magazine and the annual Billing Show, which he also developed from nothing into a world leader, Richard's *LRO* Bookshop is a treasure trove of all things Land Rover. Nowhere in the world is there such a wide selection of books and videos. The books include historical, informative, and entertaining titles on everything to do with Land Rover, with a wide choice of parts catalogues and workshop manuals for the large number of owners who look after their vehicles themselves. Richard's video library covers the same broad subject matter as the books, while for enthusiasts who want to completely immerse themselves in the part there is a very wide choice of clothing, badges, and general memorabilia.

This is one of the few places where people can get hold of prints by the celebrated artist and cartoonist, Pete Wilford, a man who fully captures the spirit of Land Rover enthusiasm in his cartoons and drawings. Enormously talented, Pete has become a celebrity in his own right in the world of Land Rovers, despite his naturally shy character. His supremely evocative drawings reflect all aspects of Land Rover life, but the characters and vehicles he depicts all come from his 30 years of involvement with the vehicles, which include many years as a successful trials competitor. As a cartoonist and illustrator he has no master.

Such is Pete's enthusiasm that he was unable to resist doing a special drawing when I told him about this book. It depicts one of Pete's great friends, Geof Miller, sorting out the problems associated with broken differentials during the Range Rover Trans Americas Expedition in 1972 (see Chapter 5).

Clubs

The following clubs operate nationally, covering all aspects of enthusiasm and every type of vehicle. Because contact names and addresses are likely to change in the lifetime of this book, it is advisable to refer to *Land Rover Owner* magazine for up-to-date information. However, relevant addresses at the time of writing (September 1998) were as follows:

All Wheel Drive Club, PO Box 320, Haywards Heath, West Sussex, RH16 3YN.

Association of Rover Clubs, John Bradbury, 14 Bolton Road, Rochdale, Lancs, OL11 4BP (01706 38801).

The Camel Club, Mrs M. M. Sweetser, The Secretary, Flat 3, 16 Drayton Green Road, West Ealing, London, W13 8RY (0181 840 4960 evenings).

Club Discovery, Warwick Banks, West Farm, Witham-on-the-Hill, Bourne, Lincs, PE10 0JN (01778 590500).

Ex-Military L-R Association, Birch Cottage, 7 Newbury Lane, Silsoe, Beds, MK45 4ET (01525 862002).

Forward Control Register IIA and IIB, 28 Front Street, Daisy Hill, Sacriston, Co Durham, DH7 6BL (0191 371 2527).

The Greenlane Association (GLASS), Shaun Seabrook, 9 Ffordd Y Dderwen, Llangewydd Court, Bridgend, Mid Glamorgan, CF31 4TQ (01656 767264 evenings).

Land Rover Owner Club, Plas-Yn-Dre, High Street, Bala, Gwynedd, LL23 7LU (0802 840444).

Land Rover Register '47–'51, Ricoli, Conisholme Road, North Somercotes, Louth, Lincs, LN11 7PS (01507 358314).

Land Rover Series I Club, David Bowyer, East Foldhay, Zeal Monachorum, Crediton, EX17 6DH (01363 82666).

Land Rover Series II Club, Frank Myatt, 8 Willow Grove, Malvern Link, Worcs, WR14 2SE.

Land Rover Series III Club, 16 Holly Street, Cannock, Staffs, WS11 2RU (01543 424821).

Lightweight Land Rover Club, Sue Foster, 31 Slimbridge Close, Breightmet, Bolton, BL2 5NT (01204 396449).

101 Forward Control Club and Register, Helena Wright, Acorn Cottage, Resting Oak Hill, Cooksbridge, Lewes, East Sussex, BN8 4PS (01273 400264 evenings).

Range Rover Register Ltd, L.J. Booth, 128 Balmoral Road, Gillingham, Kent, ME7 4QR (01634 280759, http://www.rrr.co.uk).

As well as the national clubs there are more than 100 clubs operating locally and regionally. Some are connected with national clubs, although many are independent, and a great many are members of the Association of Rover Clubs, a national body which presides over matters of major importance and/or national and international interest, and which co-ordinates off-road sporting activities.

Chapter Four

Let's go off-roading

Anybody who buys a Land Rover, no matter what type, will almost certainly want to have a go at off-roading. After all, why own a vehicle which comes from a long line of machinery designed to work over mountain, field, and forest without at least having a go? Some new owners specifically choose Land Rover because they want to become off-roaders and they know there's nothing better, but more often people will buy a leaf-sprung older Land Rover or more modern Defender, or a Discovery or Range Rover, because of the general appeal of the vehicles, and find a curiosity about off-roading develops thereafter.

This is off-roading at its most enjoyable. However, the section immediately in front of the 90 is a particularly difficult stretch with a dangerously steep fall-off on the right foreground of the picture. Areas like this should only be tackled by experts, and never alone.

The *Land Rover Owner* event at Billing is frequently the catalyst which turns new owners on to off-roading. You cannot go to the show without getting totally caught up in the enthusiasm, a great deal of which points one way or another to off-roading. And perhaps one of the strongest gauges of the degree of enthusiasm for off-roading is the fact that the off-road course at the Billing Show has to be operated on the basis of strict allocation of time slots for every hour of every day the course is open, and the entire allotment of slots is sold out months beforehand. However, it is one thing to have a Land Rover and entirely something else finding out all you need to know about off-roading.

Elsewhere in this book I have referred to the way in which greenlaning used to be the way many of us gained our off-roading experience in the past. For many there was no alternative, though I also competed in motorcycle trials for much of the 1960s, adding Land Rover craft to my two-wheel knowledge whenever I got the opportunity to drive borrowed Land Rovers on Welsh mountainsides and muddy, deeply rutted greenlanes around Northamptonshire. Information relating to the techniques of off-road driving was not available then, and neither was professional instruction – you had to learn by trial and error, and take advantage of the greater experience of others. However, the situation is very different today, and it makes good sense to study whatever you can find on the subject, and then seek out someone to provide instruction.

The specialist press publish excellent features on off-road driving techniques from time to time, and it is worth keeping an eagle eye on the magazines if you're looking for reliable, written advice of this type. The topic has also been covered in books relating to Land Rovers, so there's no excuse for not understanding at

Off-roading expeditions are as tough, or as easy, as you wish to make them. Here a Camel Trophy Freelander takes a breather during a drive along forest tracks that are well within its capabilities. (Carl Rodgerson)

least some of the basics before getting your wheels muddy for the first time. There's also a lot to be said for watching how others do it, perhaps at club off-roading events, off-roading weekends, and at the off-road course at the Billing Show. Be careful, though, because some of those you'll be watching will be people with even less knowledge than yourself; another hazard is that some drivers who have been roughing it for years can adopt an unwise and unsafe approach to difficult terrain. The greatest advantage of taking a look at people enjoying themselves in standard, road-going Land Rovers, Discoverys, and Range Rovers is that it shows you what these vehicles can cope with – which can be a surprise to the novice – and the kind of conditions they can't master, which is equally important.

But without the right technique off-roading can be dangerous, and there's a high risk of damaging your vehicle if you go about things the wrong way, even when the obstacles are not particularly difficult. For example, a simple, fairly shallow ditch, when crossed in the right way, can result in little more than a series of gentle lurches as the wheels pass through it; tackled incorrectly, at the wrong speed, the same ditch could bring you to a jarring, damaging halt, or even flip your vehicle on to its side. This is why it makes good sense to read up on the subject and then pay for a day's professional tuition with an off-road driving school before trying it out for yourself.

Land Rover Owner magazine runs a good scheme which actively encourages and assists people to enjoy off-roading on special sites, and which also offers professional guidance and tuition with one of Britain's most experienced instructors, Dave Mitchell. The *LRO* Club's driving experience days are held at selected venues around the country, always under expert supervision, while the training days provide one-to-one tuition. Full details about the club, and its activities, are published on a regular basis.

Dave Mitchell also provides instruction in off-road driving and vehicle recovery at his North Wales centre through his Landcraft organisation (01678 520820). The site, near Bala, provides a variety of challenges in a spectacular mountain setting, and from his headquarters Dave is able to provide a variety of off-road equipment, clothing, books, videos – and the world's largest choice of Land Rover models! Dave, who organises the all-

Even Range Rovers get stuck! The author and Dave Mitchell (pictured) had to rescue this Range Rover with Dave's 110 after it had become stranded on a Welsh hillside.

important marshalling arrangements for the Billing Show and numerous other events, and who has been intimately involved for many years in the ultimate off-roading event, the Welsh Hill Rally, has participated in all aspects of off-roading for many years, including trialling, in which he was once a successful competitor.

Britain's first professional, purpose-built off-road instruction course was established in Devon in the 1980s by Dave Bowyer, who has for 20 years combined the two roles of off-roading expert and 4×4 journalist. His *Overlander* magazine was the first specifically 4×4 publication in Britain. Dave enjoys an annual high-profile role as the master of ceremonies for the Billing Show's arena programme, in which he presents a non-stop mixture of events, many of which provide extremely useful advice, along with practical demonstrations of off-road driving techniques and various aspects of vehicle recovery

through the use of winches, high-lift jacks, ropes, and straps. His company, David Bowyer's Off-Road Centre (01363 82666), is able to provide instruction on a personal basis around a course which has been refined and improved over the years, and also teaches recovery techniques. Dave also organises experience-gaining greenlaning expeditions to various parts of the country, including Wales. A wide range of recovery equipment can be purchased through him.

The third of the very high-profile off-road schools is Vince Cobley's Pro Trax organisation in Northamptonshire (01536 770096). Like the others, Vince provides one-to-one tuition with himself or other highly-skilled drivers. However, he takes it further than most, and is able to offer a wide range of terrain at different locations, ranging from steep, rocky terrain in a quarry – where there's also deep water for those wanting wading experience – to mud-driving and forest trails at other sites

This 90, specially prepared by Rogers of Bedford for serious off-roading, is negotiating a deep river crossing. Unexpected riverbed holes can catch the unwary.

LEFT Although this 90 Turbo Diesel has been fitted with off-roading tyres and a Warn winch, this sort of terrain can be tackled by perfectly standard vehicles. At least one of the group should have a winch, or at the very least a tow rope.

and real-life experience on demanding mountain tracks in Wales.

Off-road training centres

There are, of course, plenty of other off-road schools, and most of them can provide expert tuition in a variety of conditions, in much the same way as the three highlighted already. All the principal ones are members of the British Off-Road Driving Association (BORDA), and most can offer training and/or experience-gaining driving sessions. Among them at the time of writing were:

Scotland
Barony College, Dumfries
   (01387 860251).
Central 4×4 Outdoor Leisure, Bo'ness,
   West Lothian (01506 516448).
Don Coyote, Edinburgh (0131 443 2881).
Glentarkie Off-Road, Strathmiglo, Fife
   (01337 860528).
Highland Off-Road, Dunkeld, Perthshire
   (01350 728700).
Highland Drovers Off-Road Driving
   Centre, Kincardine (01479 831329).
John Cockburn Off-Road, Cambusbarron,
   Stirling (01786 448356).
Newton Hill Country Sports, Fife
   (01382 542513).
Perthshire Off-Road Driving Centre,
   Dupplin, Perth (01738 633823).
Ronnie Dale Off-Road Adventure Driving
   School, Duns, Berwickshire
   (01361 840244).
Safedrive (UK) Ltd, Laurencekirk,
   Kincardineshire (01561 3789379).
Scotia Off-Road, Tibbermore, Perth
   (01764 683391).

Shandon Country Pursuits, Argyle & Bute
   (01436 820838).
Woodland Off-Road, Bellater
   (01339 755587).

Wales
Dave Mitchell's Landcraft, Bala, Gwynedd
   (01678 520820).
Forest Experience 4×4 Centre, Carno,
   Powys (01686 420201).
Motor Safari, Wrexham (01978 760679).

Northern Ireland
Northern Ireland Off-Road Centre,
   Saintfield, Co Down (01238 511763).
Safari Ireland, Enniskillen, Co Fermanagh
   (01365 322588).
Todds Leap, Ballygawley, Co Tyrone
   (01868 758155).

England
Battle Off-Road Centre, Battle, Sussex
   (01424 870847).
Benniworth Springs Academy of Off-Road
   Driving, Benniworth, Lincs
   (01507 313682).
Bishop Burton College, Beverley, East
   Yorks (01964 553000).
Bradley Off-Road Ltd, Maiden Bradley,
   Wilts (01985 844844).
Cheviot 4×4 Centre, Wooler,
   Northumberland (01668 282287).
David Bowyer's Off-Road Centre,
   Crediton, Devon (01363 82666).
Devils Pit, Luton, Beds (01582 883349).
Drive & Survive UK, Crowthorne, Berks
   (01344 751177).
Edge Hill Shooting Ground & 4×4,
   Banbury, Oxon (01925 678141).
Everyman Driving Centre, Mallory Park
   Racing Circuit, Leics (01455 841670).
Fennes Off-Road Driving School,
   Braintree, Essex (01376 342695).
Folly 4×4, Marlborough, Wilts
   (01264 731456).
Fresh Tracks, Ware, Herts
   (01920 438758).

Golding Barn 4×4 Off-Road Driving
Centre & Chichester Off-Road
Adventures, Steyning, Sussex
(01903 812195).

Ian Wright Off-Road Driving School,
Haywards Heath, Sussex
(01444 881190).

Lakeland Safari, Broughton in Furness,
Cumbria (01229 716943).

Leisure Pursuits, East Grinstead, Sussex
(01342 825522).

Manby Performance Driving Centre,
Louth, Lincs (01507 601652).

Manor House Leisure Ltd, Saltburn,
Cleveland (01947 840944).

March Hare Leisure Centre, nr Worcester
(01905 381219).

Mid Norfolk Off-Road Centre, Runhall,
Norwich (01362 850233).

The Mud Factory, East Grinstead, Sussex
(01342 315504).

North Herefordshire Off-Road Driving
School, Marden, Hereford
(01568 797372).

North Yorkshire Off-Road Centre, Robin
Hood's Bay, North Yorks
(01947 880371).

Northants 4×4, Grafton Underwood,
Northants (01536 330222).

Off-Road Motivations, Andover, Wilts
(01264 710113).

Off-Road Pursuits, Chester
(0700 944834).

Off-Road Rovers, Penzance, Cornwall
(01252 311075).

Off Trax 4×4 Driving Centre,
Brentwood, Essex (01277 214273).

Pro-Trax, Northants (01536 770096).

Quest 4×4, Rudgwick, Sussex
(01403 822439).

Reading Trail Park, Reading, Berks
(0118 9314976).

Spectrum 4×4, Barnsley, South Yorks
(01226 748822).

Team Mudplugging, Tonbridge, Kent
(01634 271860).

Three Counties Driver Training,
Newthorpe, Nottingham
(0115 9385561).

Tuf-Trax, West Haddon, Northants
(01788 510575).

Venture 4×4 Off-Road Driving Centre,
Wisbech, Cambs (01945 772270).

Weardale Off-Road Centre, Wolsingham,
Co Durham (01388 527375).

Whitecliffe Off-Road School, Forest of
Dean (01594 834666).

Wild Tracks, Newmarket, Suffolk
(01638 751918).

Wildrovers (Worldwide), Stockport,
Cheshire (0161 449 0725).

Yorkshire 4×4 Exploration, Exelby,
North Yorks (01677 427222).

Please note that the above details may
change, and it pays to keep an eye on the
Land Rover enthusiast press for up-to-date
information.

Learning from experts

What can you expect to learn at an off-
road driving school? Indeed, is it worth
the expense of taking professional tuition
when it is surely possible to pick it up as
you go along? The most important lessons
to be learned are that there is more to
driving off-road than meets the eye, that
it can be dangerous, yet can be enjoyed
without either danger or damage, and that
recovery techniques are an important part
of the activity. While the theory relating
to all this can be picked up by reading
about it – and, indeed, the written word
should be the starting point for all novices
– there is no substitute for instruction
behind the wheel.

A typical course for somebody new to
off-roading would include:

– a classroom session, in which the use of
the transfer box, for normal or low
gear ratios, is explained, along with the
reason for the centre differential and

The editor of Land Rover Owner *magazine, Carl Rodgerson, attaches a towing strap prior to rescuing the author, who had got this Series IIA stuck on an unexpectedly steep ridge. Basic equipment like this can save a very long walk.*

This Defender is equipped for every off-roading eventuality, with a top-quality Warn winch and front recovery attachment.

the benefits of using its locking facility; understanding wheel articulation; use of the clutch; the importance of proceeding slowly and 'reading' the way ahead; throttle control; vehicle limitations; the use of seat belts; and general safety considerations;

– a basic driving session, getting the feel of the vehicle and engine in low ratios; using the controls; clutch and throttle technique; holding the steering wheel correctly; 'reading' the position of the front wheels; simple climbs and descents; and experiencing side slopes;

– progression to more difficult climbs and descents; rutted tracks; mud techniques; coping with rocks; basic wading techniques; and crossing ditches;

– more advanced climbs and difficult descents; failed hill climb techniques;

deep mud; deep wading; understanding guidance signals; and difficult reversing.

From this point it becomes important to learn how to use vehicle-mounted winches for recovery, with special emphasis on the aspects relating to safety, the use of ground anchors, high-lift jacks, towed recovery techniques, kinetic recovery, and the role of all related equipment. These more advanced matters are usually covered in follow-up sessions and, for effective understanding, need plenty of practice time.

Naturally, the various schools approach off-road training in their own way, paying due heed to the abilities of the student and their desired requirements from the course. If someone wishes, for example, to know how to cope with a horse-box in wet fields (not as easy as it sounds) that's

Vince Cobley of the Pro-Trax school in Northamptonshire explains the perils of tackling a rutted downhill section with the steering turned across the ruts.

The combination of restricted suspension movement, limited ground clearance, and the lack of separate low ratios restricts the Freelander's off-roading capability. In this demonstration the vehicle was unable to conquer this simple gully section.

Vince Cobley explains how not to tackle a ditch crossing in such a way that the front of the Discovery becomes stuck. Crossed obliquely the ditch would present no difficulty.

fine, but at the other end of the scale people come along seeking training for trans-Sahara expeditions and for working in the African bush.

Schools will also provide advice on the best choice of tyres for an individual's particular circumstances, along with other equipment such as side protectors, winches, jacks, ropes, wading equipment and preparation, and lighting. However, it also helps to keep an eye on the sort of equipment other people are using, and the way they prepare their vehicles. This is where joining either a local or national club appropriate to your vehicle and interests is extremely worthwhile; listening to experienced enthusiasts talking about their own vehicles and, sometimes, the mistakes they have made, helps to keep you on the straight and narrow yourself, whether you own a battered Series II or a sparkling new Range Rover.

Off-roading is great fun which, through making full use of a Land Rover's enormous capabilities, opens up an entirely new world of motoring. But please remember:

– Be safe at all times.
– Tread lightly wherever you go.
– Never go where you shouldn't.
– Never venture off-road unprepared.
– Fully understand your vehicle and its limitations.
– Never damage the terrain, wildlife, or plants.

Happy off-roading!

Chapter Five

Range Rover: the inside story of a world-beater

The Range Rover was the most important vehicle to be produced by Land Rover – apart, that is, from the first generation of Land Rovers. It was a vehicle which enhanced profoundly the fortunes of Rover and did more than any other product to raise the general public's awareness of off-road machinery. No other vehicle combined so effectively the Range Rover's unique mixture of performance, comfort, usefulness, and truly outstanding off-road capability.

The Range Rover managed to break away from the traditionalist approach which had prevailed at Land Rover, and which continued with the utility models right through to the end of Series III production, 15 years after the Range Rover's launch. In breaking the mould it pioneered transmission and suspension technology which, eventually, would be used for the 110 and 90, and around which the supremely successful Discovery would be constructed. Without the Range Rover there is every possibility that Land Rover might have become one of the many failures of the British motor industry, instead of being an unrivalled success. Range Rover was, and is, one of the very few genuine landmark vehicles of motoring history.

As with many entirely new vehicles it is quite difficult to find a point in time which was the true beginning of the Range Rover. It can be just as difficult to pinpoint exactly *why* it was decided to produce a particular vehicle in the first place and, again, this is true of the Range Rover. It has been said in the past that the inspiration for the Range Rover was market research conducted in America, but while it is true that Rover was looking keenly at the situation in the USA relating to vehicles with off-road capability – as opposed to true off-road machinery as we generally understand it in Great Britain today – there were many other factors which led, directly or otherwise, to the Range Rover.

One of the very few people who was involved with the Range Rover project from an early stage was Geof Miller, who worked as Project Engineer, Range Rover from 1966. Geof, a highly skilled engineer, joined Rover originally as Technical Assistant, Land Rover Engineering. He became so immersed in the job that it spilled over into his private life, leading to him becoming one of the earliest Land Rover enthusiasts. This was a passion which was to endure, and today he is a familiar sight at Land Rover events throughout Britain with his two Range Rovers – a pre-production Velar and an EFi.

Geof witnessed every aspect of the

This publicity photograph was taken in preparation for the launch of the Range Rover in June 1970. (Rover Group/BMIHT/National Motor Museum)

LEFT The three ages of the Range Rover. In the foreground is one of the very earliest models (the same vehicle is also seen in the next photograph), in the centre is one of the last of the original models, and at the back is the all-new model launched in 1994. (National Motor Museum)

By the time the LSE came along the Range Rover had become a sophisticated vehicle, as this cutaway of the 1992 LSE clearly demonstrates. (National Motor Museum)

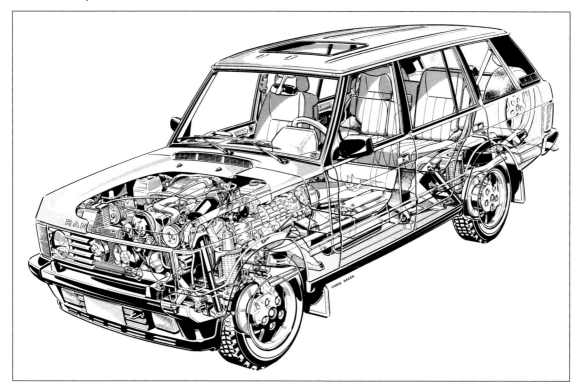

development of the Range Rover project first-hand, and in the exclusive interview with the author related here he tells the full story leading up to the launch in 1970. It makes fascinating reading, not least because it is a story which has never been told before in such detail, nor with such intimate, behind-the-scenes insight. His account reveals quite a few secrets, nails a few myths, and shows just how inspired the development team was, despite the fact that until Geof took the entire crew on an off-roading exercise he was the only member of the Range Rover project team who had driven off-road. Indeed, many of them had never even driven a Land Rover before!

From quick sketches to Range Rover

as told by project development engineer, Geof Miller

It is difficult to know where to start, really, but because Rover had concluded what was to prove an historically significant deal with Buick, which led to us having the perfect engine for the Range Rover, it seems sensible to look back at the engine situation.

A V6 engine was, I believe, part of the deal with Buick which transferred the manufacturing rights of the now-familiar V8 engine to Rover, and we were performance testing 88-inch Land Rovers in Autumn 1964 fitted with a Buick cast iron 3.5-litre V6 against the Rover straight six 3-litre and the P6 2-litre overhead cam unit. My understanding is that as part of the deal – part of the box of parts William Martin-Hurst brought back from the States in the very early stages of the deal with Buick – were some Buick V8 engines and possibly a small batch of their cast iron V6 units. It is possible that as

well as us having one at Land Rover, the car section may have had one or, perhaps more likely, the engine development section probably put one on a test bed.

We didn't like the weight of the V6 but it probably had slightly better low-speed torque characteristics than the V8. We played about with various differential ratios and the figures we got were masked to some extent by the gearing differences, but there wouldn't have been a great deal in it in overall terms. Tested in an 88-inch in the middle of 1965, we did find it slightly better at low engine speeds than either of the other two engines on test at the time.

Then very soon after that we began to assemble the three 88-inch prototypes with early build versions of the Buick aluminium V8 which eventually came into production. These were built in late-1965 and we were testing the engines into 1966, when I was still working as Project Engineer, Basic Vehicles, which included all 88s and 109s of all body varieties, plus the new six-cylinder 109 that we were developing for the States. This was a station wagon in left-hand drive only, and the engine was the car unit which we developed initially for the USA, but then brought in as a regular model later on.

Then in June 1966 I moved over to the Range Rover project, and took those three very important vehicles with me. Two of these had manual transmission and one was an automatic. One of these is now at the Dunsfold Museum, and started its life in a pale blue Rover P6 car colour and was prepared for doing 100,000 miles of road endurance work, because it was a serious project at one stage with the V8 engine. Martin-Hurst wanted to bring that in as a production vehicle, but by the time we'd got the vehicle prepared to do the mileage endurance test we had convinced him that the gearbox and clutch of an 88 wasn't up to the V8 power, and so the project was cancelled. That particular pale blue vehicle was then adapted for other work, and it ended up as a tow vehicle for a skid trailer for measuring the friction levels on road surfaces. It was resprayed red, and that is how it now is at Dunsfold.

The intention had been, even that early, to produce V8 Land Rovers. We went through two phases of expanding the range with new vehicles. One was to go back to a small, basic 80-inch type vehicle with the Rover 2000 engine, and that was dropped; then we went to the other end of the scale where we took an 88-inch Land Rover and looked into giving it high power. This is where the competition was coming from with the Japanese – Toyota and Nissan – who had introduced what were very similar vehicles to an 88-inch Land Rover, but with 3- or 4-litre power. And this enabled them to make gains over Land Rover.

Our efforts to get more power were still being based on getting 55bhp out of a two-and-a-quarter instead of 52bhp! All of which was ludicrous in the face of 4-litre straight six engines with over a hundred horse power, which was the background to Martin-Hurst wanting to put the newly-acquired 3.5-litre V8 into an ordinary Land Rover. Unfortunately, this was the worst vehicle to start with because the 88-inch Land Rover didn't have the strength of components for that sort of torque. But we had still pushed ahead before convincing him with paper calculations that it was a non-starter.

Start of the project

At the time of the cancellation of the original plan for a high-power Land Rover I was told about the project for the Interim Station Wagon, destined to become the Range Rover, and was promptly transferred. An interesting point

Geof Miller and his wife pose with their much-loved Velar at the Billing Show. Geof was intimately involved with the engineering development of the project from the mid-1960s, and was the only Land Rover enthusiast connected with the work.

is whether this had ever been seen as a long-term project. Because the military situation at the time was causing substantial reductions in orders a very large production gap needed filling. Clearly, we wanted to do something about it and take up the spare production capacity. As ever, people started to say that we needed a new vehicle, thinking, apparently, that we could come up with one in just a few months. Of course, this wasn't the case, but while all this was going on it was a fact that people were looking at something entirely different.

It is definitely not true that Range Rover came about just as an expedient stop-gap. There were three independent lines of enquiry going along at the same time. Firstly, there was the gap-filling exercise brought about by the drop in military business. Secondly, market research were looking at the American market and seeing what was happening there in the way of leisure vehicles. Thirdly, Spen King, having designed the Rover 2000, didn't have a great deal of work on his plate, and with people talking enthusiastically about the vastly improved quality of ride and handling of the new P6 car, he started to look at the idea of taking the lessons learned from that vehicle and applying them to a Land Rover.

These three things rather knitted together to give the idea of coming up with a vehicle that filled the production capacity gap, but also moved forward in design parameters and hopefully would appeal to a new market – North America – which was exploding into leisure activity. Evidence of that came in the International Scout and the Ford Bronco; the Americans had always had a leisure motoring situation with things such as the Jeep Wagonaire and Cherokee, a big road-based station wagon with some off-road capability, but they wanted more. Of course, off-road ability in their sense meant being able to cope with gravel and dirt roads, rather than the outright cross-country capability which we mean when talking about off-roading. The Americans had started to come down from large vehicles like the Cherokee, as it was then, and other big machines, more towards Land Rover size, like the Scout and the Bronco.

The influence of the Rover P6

It is difficult to be absolutely precise about the state of the Range Rover project when I was first involved in it. Spen King and Gordon Bashford had certainly been looking at the situation for some months

because I can remember, probably in late-1965, some of Gordon's people wanting to borrow an 88-inch Land Rover to look at, and we started to wonder what the hell they were looking at Land Rovers for. Apart from Gordon having been involved in the very first Land Rovers in 1948, he and Spen had been involved exclusively in car design; but they were definitely showing keen interest when they borrowed that 88-inch.

Spen and Gordon had started to think about the application of Rover 2000 levels of ride comfort and interior trim applied to a Land Rover, and Gordon Bannock – who was the marketing guy engaged by William Martin-Hurst to look at the situation in the USA and other areas, primarily Africa and Asia, to see what was happening in the 4×4 market and what we needed to look at – came up with some ideas.

In the meeting I have in mind, Spen suddenly said, 'Something like this you mean?' and both of them were staggered that they had come up with similar ideas, one from the marketing viewpoint and the other from engineering. This was an estate car, with car standards of interior comfort and ride comfort. They weren't necessarily thinking of coil springs at that time – bear in mind that all Land Rovers then were on leaf springs – but it very quickly settled in that direction. Spen's basic idea was long travel and low rate suspension, to have plenty of movement available at low rate, whereas all Land Rovers had high rate springs and short travel, giving them their characteristically hard ride. And this was to be applied to an off-road vehicle, a revolutionary way of thinking.

Land Rover people had always said before this that it wasn't the way to do things because if you gave the driver too much comfort he would break the vehicle. Tom Barton used to, and still does, boast that you protected the vehicle by the degree of discomfort that the driver suffered. So Spen wasn't, at least to begin with, looking specifically at coil springs. But, of course, the P6 did have coil springs, and the P6 was his baby. Inevitably, of course, coil springing was among the first things they looked at, along with advanced (for those days) leaf spring designs – single leaf, tapered leaf, and various others. However, these were abandoned for this project in favour of coil springs.

It is interesting, by the way, that the Japanese went for leaf springs in their off-roaders of the early and mid-1980s, some 20 years after the period we're talking about. In some ways they did it a little better in that they had more travel, giving better comfort and a bit more off-road ability with quite good articulation. But what they tended not to do was to have ride control ability; while they had a better starting point and potentially better ability, they failed to make the most of it.

Getting the package together

Initially, on the Range Rover, there was Spen King, Gordon Bashford, his deputy Joe Brown, and two section leaders – Phil Banks, who was a chassis engineer, and a body engineer named Phil Jackson. They started to look at, basically, sketches on pads, and that developed so that by the time I was moved into Spen and Gordon's area in July 1966 they had schemes on paper. They were then struggling with getting the package together to get what's known as the 95th percentile male, the average big guy, in a P6 seat with P6 comfort, P6 steering position, positioned comfortably in the car, with back seats and rear load area, a bulkhead in front of him with some engine area. They were working on all this and had looked at a 2.25-litre Land Rover engine and a 3-litre car engine, and were then told to put the V8 in.

Probably three weeks to a month after I joined them they were in the situation to say that with the V8 engine in the front, and fitting everything else around it, this would be the vehicle; it needed a wheelbase of 99.5 inches, a height of 70 inches and a width of 70 inches and they could achieve all of the physical standards they were looking for relative to design layout and occupant space and comfort.

While it was assumed from very early on that it would have two doors, it was going to be a five passenger, car-type interior, with no sideways-facing seats or anything like that. There would be two or three front seats and a two or three person bench seat in the back, plus a payload area. It meant it would be a fairly large vehicle, but it needn't have been quite so long with such a pronounced rear overhang behind the rear axle; but having got it pretty well sorted from radiator to rear axle it was already a biggish car, and therefore there was no point in having a tiny load area at the back. We wanted sufficient luggage space for five occupants to go continental touring.

This basic design phase was around July and August 1966, and the first body came along probably towards the middle of 1967, but in the meantime, having got the overall shape that they wanted, it was then a case of designing the shape of the shell to cover it up, and at this stage styling were tied up with other projects. Spen and Gordon were doing this particular project because they had finished one or two others and weren't occupied on other things. Dave Bache was under the direction of the main Board on other matters, so he was very reluctant to pick up anything on the Range Rover, or the Interim Station Wagon as it was still being known. He was just too busy. Consequently, it was left to Spen, Gordon and Phil Jackson to decide what the body would look like. I think Phil in particular was one of the background heroes of this project, and he dealt with what we knew as the jig shop, who were the experts in panel beating and fabrication. Literally with sketches on cigarette packets and chalk drawings on the floor he got the men in the jig shop to make up the first body. Believe it or not, this is how the Range Rover's body shape came into being.

This initial body shape became reality with the first prototype, which was built in the summer and autumn of 1967. That design was subsequently tidied up by Dave Bache, and tidying up was all that was involved, although to anyone other than Dave it would still have been a major challenge. The proportions were all there, the outline was there, and when you look at that first body alongside the final version you can see Dave's skill in the way he took what was a pretty ordinary looking body, with the right dimensions and features, and gave it the 26-year production life it was destined to have. It achieved genuine classic status in its own lifetime, from such humble beginnings.

The only 4×4 expert on the project

My prime task when I moved on to the project was to give everyone the background 4×4 knowledge which was otherwise lacking. Perhaps surprisingly, I was the only 4×4 expert on the entire Range Rover project. Whereas in the Land Rover development area a lot of the people involved were interested in 4×4s themselves and had their own vehicles, as I did, in the New Vehicle Project area they were designers. Nobody in the design

The Range Rover has always been very popular with the police. Here is a very early police conversion, with exceptionally large sign in the special roof modification which also housed beacons and floodlights. (National Motor Museum)

office had owned or, in most cases, had ever driven a Land Rover, so one of the first things I had to do was to get together a large assortment of Land Rovers and competitive vehicles and take them down to Eastnor Castle. Then I had to take all the New Projects design people, plus engine design and transmission design staff, on a demanding safari around Eastnor Castle.

We had set up a 13-mile off-road course around Eastnor and it took two days to cover it. This was very much throwing all these key people into the deep end of off-roading; Eastnor in November can be pretty grim, so much so that several years later when I was in the Panamanian jungle with the Trans Americas Expedition I described the conditions in the jungle as 'just like Eastnor in November'. They were able to drive some of the vehicles down to Eastnor and back. The variety of machinery was impressive: standard 88s, 109s, Forward Controls, the V8 engined 88-inch, V6 88-inch, Nissan Patrol, Ford Bronco, International Scout, Haflinger, and more. The opportunity for everybody involved to drive them in all sorts of conditions – ranging from quite mild off-road to extremely severe – was invaluable. Most importantly, they came back understanding fully what they were trying to achieve.

Getting the suspension sorted

From that point they were then detailing the whole of the vehicle. We built Prototype No 1, took it to Eastnor and found that in general terms it fulfilled Spen and Gordon's requirements for ride quality, speed, ability, and comfort (to a degree), but it was lacking in handling. The suspension that they'd drawn up wasn't right in practice.

At that time we were not using permanent four-wheel drive, but conventional Land Rover type transmission mated to a 'Roverised' Buick V8 engine. Various suspension arrangements had been looked at in the early stages; despite the influence of the P6 in some areas, that car's de Dion rear suspension, which helps give it such excellent ride and handling, had been discounted early on because of the lack of movement of the differential. We'd stuck with beam axles for all the right reasons. Explained simply, it had what was really something like the Ford Bronco suspension, and having tried it, and found it lacking, we then looked at it critically and decided that we never would be able to make it work as we wanted it to.

Spen stated straight away, 'We're not accepting that. We're going to re-do the rear suspension.' In fact, it was the location of the axles which was not working, and so they went back to the drawing board and came up with their own principles of fairly straightforward systems of leading arm or trailing arm location of the axles, with a Panhard rod at the front and an A-frame located over the centre of the axle at the rear. No 2 prototype was then put into the system with this method of axle location and was built in early-1968. We just managed to get this vehicle on the road for Spen to try around the test track before he was moved away from Rover, in one of the British Leyland reorganisations, and given the job of Technical Director at Triumph.

The fact that Spen was able to find the right suspension arrangement was to prove crucial to the Range Rover, which in turn eventually led to the complete family of coil-sprung Land Rover vehicles. Spen rightfully takes the credit, along with Gordon Bashford, for the overall design of the vehicle. Spen was the sort of active brain behind it, and Gordon was the man who transposed Spen's ideas on to paper and then passed it on in very schematic form to Joe Brown and the rest of the team, who put it into detail and were able to get it built.

In that redesign, the vehicle didn't have a rear levelling device and between the time it was built and tested, and the redesign of its suspension, Spen and Gordon had been to a motor show in Germany and seen the Mercedes suspension with a Boge levelling unit. They realised that on the Range Rover it would fit perfectly with the new A-frame rear axle location and provide self-levelling suspension. This would, we realised, be a real step forward in the area of allowable spring rates and general ride, because it

One of the earliest five-speed Range Rovers was this one, used by the author over an extended period from new. A210 SGN was a long-term test vehicle for Motor, *of which the author was publisher.*

permits softer springing and gives, in effect, a three-spring arrangement at the rear of the vehicle. Spen and Gordon then designed this levelling unit into the Mk 2 suspension.

Moving to permanent 4×4

In the meantime, we had had worries about the amount of power and torque available, in relation to axle strength and handling, and so we had taken two of the 88-inch V8s and left one with the standard Land Rover part-time four-wheel drive transmission. Now, we just happened to have in the stores a permanent four-wheel drive type gearbox with a centre differential which we had been playing about with earlier on the 88-inch vehicles. It was a design which had been tried and put aside, so we fetched this gearbox out and fitted it to the second 88. This enabled us to compare two 88s – one with conventional part-time four-wheel drive and the other with permanent four-wheel drive – and we liked what we saw.

So, into the specification of the second prototype we put permanent four-wheel drive. This vehicle was prepared with the improved suspension, Girling disc brakes (as opposed to the drums on the first one and the Lockheed system with which we went into production), and the revised transmission. But it still had the No 1 body style. This vehicle was driven by Spen before he departed for Triumph, and he was happy that he had overcome most, if not all, of the problems which we had found on No 1.

In the chassis design we applied all the principles we had learned with Land Rovers, with side rails which were adequately strong, if not too strong, with cross members in the right place, so that the general principles of a Land Rover chassis were followed. But the Range

Rover chassis was going to be two U-shaped channels welded together rather than four plates. We had phases of quality problems with Land Rover chassis, and the basic method of construction had always been something of a worry, because it doesn't provide the strongest result. With the Range Rover we had wanted to get away from that, so we had decided on the double U-section construction. The general idea was that this would be a vertical U and an inverted U welded together along the neutral axis, but in fact it proved difficult to do that, so we ended up with two channels put together sideways and welded along the top and bottom, with the welds back in the areas we didn't like. However, we felt we could cope with that on a production basis much better than what was first specified. The attachments and brackets, engine mounts, suspension mounts and things like that were new, because we were using coil springs with location arms.

We carried on with development work and eventually we endurance tested that No 2 prototype at MIRA on the pavé and cross country routes. We did what we know as a double pavé test. Normally, the pavé test consisted of 1,500 miles, a mix of pavé and cross country, unladen, half-laden, and fully-laden; but on anything new this was doubled up just to make sure that everything was as it should be, and this is what happened on No 2. We found one or two problems and put them right, so that by the time No 3 was being specified we'd got the chassis sorted, we knew what we wanted in suspension, transmission and braking, and Dave Bache had tidied up the body.

This meant that No 3 prototype, which was left-hand drive and Lincoln green, was built about the end of 1968, as it would look in production and as it would be specified in production. The rest of the prototypes, Nos 4, 5, 6 and 7, were built

This is prototype Velar number 6 on general development testing. (Geof Miller)

to that specification, and then we went into pre-production.

The phantom pick-up

Although there were not too many diversions once the actual project was rolling, there was the case of the Range Rover pick-up that never was, which was the direct cause of part of the Range Rover's great chassis strength. Late one evening in the earlier stages when we'd got the fundamental layout sorted, William Martin-Hurst came into the office to get a progress report. We went through everything with him and he seemed to be quite pleased. Then he turned round and dropped a bombshell on everyone by saying, 'Is that all OK now if we decide to make a pick-up as well as a station wagon?' About six jaws dropped in unison as we looked at each other, while we all had the same thought: 'Nobody said anything about a pick-up.'

Next morning Joe Brown and the design engineer sat down with Alan Ancliffe, the stress engineer, did a load of sums, and carried on with the idea that if there was a possibility of having a payload-carrying pick-up, as opposed to a people-carrying station wagon, perhaps we ought to increase the size of the chassis in the points of worst bending moment, which was basically the centre section of the chassis beneath the front seats. Consequently we added an extra half-inch to the depth of the chassis frame in this area; of course, we never built a pick-up, so this extra strength which was designed in from Day 2 as opposed to Day 1, amounted to over-engineering, but it adds to the long life of the chassis, and has probably been a good thing over the years.

On top of this episode, Spen and Gordon stuck to a two-door vehicle in the initial design, partly because the Americans were building two-door vehicles, and partly because they were a little concerned about the risks of going to a four-door body in the very early stages, in that a four-door body would inevitably be somewhat weaker than a two-door. Consequently we were going only for the safe option of a two-door. When it came to the crunch and we built the first body and did some stiffness tests on it, it was obviously far superior to the bitsa-type body which goes on a Land Rover, which has no integral strength of its own. In contrast, the Range Rover body had a lot of integral strength, so that by the time you've mounted the Range Rover body on to an already stronger chassis you have a heck of a strong vehicle. Again, this has

paid dividends over the years, but we knew even before we began testing that we had a good, strong assembly.

The first vehicle I referred to earlier was really only a mobile running bed rather than a test bed. The second vehicle had somewhere near correct running gear, which enabled us to do a lot of the endurance and performance testing, transmission and brake assessment on the second vehicle to be built, which is quite an achievement really. Then as soon as No 3 vehicle came along with the right body and correct gearbox type we were well on the way. And, of course, while these things were going on the transmission people were designing a brand-new gearbox. We knew the Land Rover gearbox wasn't strong enough and the 9-inch clutch wasn't big enough, so we were designing in a big, hefty, four-speed gearbox with a new transfer box, a bigger transmission brake and a 9.5-inch diaphragm spring clutch rather than the smaller, standard type of clutch.

'Roverising' the big Buick

All these transmission-related things were going on in the background, while the engine people were increasing the 'Roverisation' of the Buick engine. The first engine we used was very much a Buick complete with a Buick carburettor, with modified exhaust manifolds. The second engine was more 'Roverised' in that it initially had SU carburettors (as in its car application), although we would be going eventually on to Strombergs. We needed a raised water pump and fan position, different sump, and different compression ratio. Therefore as we moved from prototype No 1 to No 2 and then No 3, the transmission came more up-to-date, as did the brakes, and the engine moved forward and became closer to what we saw as the production specification.

At Rover we always had an engine design section and an engine development section, so they were told what we wanted in the way of water pump and fan position relative to our radiator mounting position, etc, with the right engine mounts, and the sump shaped to clear the front axle. There were Land Rover and car sides of the engine development section, and they were modifying the engines to the sort of specification we wanted, and then testing the engines on test beds, working out power curves and so on.

We ended up with Stromberg carburettors because the Stromberg had the float chamber concentric with the needle, and therefore regardless of which way you tilted the vehicle the carburation was unaffected. With the offset float chambers of the SU, tilting the vehicle one way starves the carburettor of petrol, while tilting it the other floods it, which is not a lot of good with an off-road machine. The American carburettors were hopeless; if you went fast round a bend you either flooded or starved the engine. So we went for Strombergs, running with a compression ratio of 8.1:1; in the very early stages it was 8.25:1, whereas the P5 cars, which were the first to actually use the Buick V8 engine, were over 10:1.

Although it was conceived as an interim, stop-gap product, our vehicle was going to have the Land Rover name on it, and so it had to be able to do all the things that Land Rovers did, and that meant going world-wide, which in turn meant being able to use cheap, inferior petrol. That was why we had to downrate the compression ratio compared with the car, the actual ratio changing over the years and ending up, I think, at 8.13:1. As a point of interest my own understanding of some of these changes was that it wasn't the actual ratio that changed, it was just the figure which changed because the mathematicians had made a miscalculation! The story I got was that it was put out as being 8.25 when it should have been 8.13.

This all meant we were pursuing our own course, compared with the car people at Rover, when it came to water pumps, fans, carburettors, sump shape, and oil filter position, again because of front axle clearance problems. Also, the carburettors and air cleaners, inlet and exhaust manifolds were all going to be different to the car.

Climate testing – a first for Land Rover

After using development engines initially, with ongoing changes, we later started to get correct specification engines which we were able to put in the vehicles and finalise our testing programmes. Part of our development testing were the various climate – hot and cold – trials. I wasn't involved in the cold weather tests in Norway, carried out in Rover's favourite cold weather test area. It is interesting that Land Rovers had not previously been cold tested as part of a development programme; all their testing had been done as the models evolved and by owners using them to do the work they'd been bought to do. But with Range Rover being a brand new vehicle (as opposed to the company's usual evolutionary development) the whole situation was different, and we had to go and do these tests.

The car people were running a test in the winter of 1968–69 and we sent a Range Rover with two or three cars – with Roger Crathorne in charge of the Range Rover, along with one of the engine development engineers – to do the cold testing. The format is always the same over the two or three week period of a cold test. You 'soak' the vehicles overnight in the lowest temperatures possible, aiming to find night temperatures of minus 30° to minus 40° whenever possible. Then, early in the morning, you follow a standardised start-up and drive-away routine, along with driving procedures and heater testing. Having the Range Rover with the cars proved useful in that it was a back-up and tow vehicle where necessary, and it performed very well. We were always surprised at how good the V8 engine was in respect of cold-starting, an experience repeated when the time came to carry out similar tests on the V8 SD1 car. Quite simply, we just didn't have any problems.

There are, of course, standard procedures for testing everything at home, either in the factory, on the roads, or on proving grounds such as MIRA. With the Range Rover, all the testing started locally until we found problems. But the hot weather testing was always going to be more of a worry than the cold tests. The problem is that the V8 engine is a bit of a lump compared with the 2.25 engines we were used to, and it develops a lot of heat, particularly at tickover. We knew we were going to face a problem of engine cooling at high temperatures.

The tests in this country were normally done at MIRA, where we did high-speed running around the test track to find what happens to temperatures, followed by low-speed slogging, towing a dynamometer, which is like towing a caravan with the brakes on and gives continuous high-torque running. Then there was another high-torque test where a dynamometer was towed round in tight circles, getting rid of any wind effects, where the vehicle is run on peak torque for as long as it takes to reach boiling point.

In most of these tests the Range Rover was equal to a Land Rover (renowned for its resistance to overheating), but where we ran into trouble was just sitting at tickover, reproducing traffic jam situations in which you're taking in other cars'

exhausts as you do in a hot city. In the UK and with standard procedures we got away with it, but we knew that with different engine specifications, such as the de-toxed engine for North America, we were going to have a problem. Therefore, we decided that for cooling and various other reasons, including internal temperatures, we had got to take the vehicle abroad to hot, ambient temperatures to make sure we could achieve the same standards as the Land Rover.

Quick trip across the Sahara

We started to think about going to Morocco and Spain where we could get ambients of at least 30° to 35°. But this was rather overtaken by circumstances, in that, with the launch coming up – because Lord Stokes was insisting that we must launch at a point that we considered to be rather early – all we could fit in was a sort of mini expedition across Algeria and Morocco. This involved two Range Rovers, a special test bed vehicle (a 109 with increased load capacity and Range Rover drive train) and a standard 109 as back-up. This was operated for us by Mini Trek, who ran holidays across Algeria and Morocco, and provided all the ground services for us.

The expedition served two purposes. It was partly an engineering exercise, and partly a filming trip for Rover's marketing operation later on. We did lots of testing on cooling temperatures, brake wear, general suspension, and ride and handling work. The film crew made very good use of the trip and created the launch film, *A Car for all Reasons*, as well as a travelogue film, *Sahara South*.

This was an initial run for conditions of this type and proved quite successful. We had one or two problems, including breaking a bracket holding the leveller on a rear axle which we had to weld up

The only hot weather testing done prior to the launch of the Range Rover was an expedition to the Sahara. Here the group stops for a break and some checks on the vehicles. (Geof Miller)

One of the Range Rovers tested in the Sahara was prototype No 5, very heavily loaded with filming equipment. Here it is parked in front of the V8 109-inch Land Rover which accompanied the Range Rovers. (Geof Miller)

there and then, but the design was modified on return and never gave any more trouble. From that trip in November–December 1969 we sussed out where to go in Morocco to get the right conditions, so that in the summer of 1970 we took two vehicles back to Morocco for hot testing. This was, of course, after the launch, and we did a whole load of general development work, but mainly engine and transmission cooling, plus high-speed work. These tests were especially interesting, in that we were able to prove that the basic specification was valid, but the American spec with the de-tox engine was risky. This was one of the things, among many others, which caused the cancellation of the entry into the USA market. The American standards were moving faster than we were.

In those days, expertise on reduced emissions was very limited. We could achieve the right level of exhaust cleanliness by messing about with engine timing and running the carburettors very weak at the bottom end. As with cooling, which is always a problem when idling, the worst pollution usually occurs at tickover. They wanted to run the carburettors very weak, so they wanted to get heat in there to help, which meant air mixer boxes taking warmed air in from the exhaust in some circumstances and cool air at other times. It was also necessary to vary the timing, so instead of a single vacuum actuator on the distributor we had a twin, two-way actuator, so you could pull on a lot of retard at tickover which helped clean up the exhaust, which had the effect of giving the engine a running condition it didn't like. This gave rise to a lot more heat being generated, and this in turn was boiling the water.

The engine people started to look at this, with more blades on the fan and/or increasing the fan speed, but it was a

During the cooling tests in the desert the Range Rovers were run at high speed and then parked for long periods with the engines idling. Here the bonnet of YVB 175H has been removed as part of the tests, while a local watches with interest. (Geof Miller)

losing battle really for the American market. Australia and Sweden tended to follow America closely, so we knew that in abandoning the American spec we were laying up trouble in other areas. But it really should be put into perspective, because it was only part of the American story.

Elsewhere we found that we were OK, and we didn't have any problems with the basic engine set-up or basic tune. We did further tests later on, particularly relevant to engine oil temperatures, testing with and without an oil cooler. Generally speaking we found we could get by without an oil cooler; certain conditions required it, but this requirement was satisfied by offering it as an option. It was only ever fitted as standard with automatic transmission.

The next stage for me after the launch was to help out with a kind of second check for a potentially big market which existed in South Africa, and it led to me taking two Range Rovers out to Cape Town on what amounted to a combined marketing and engineering exercise. This was in February–March 1971, and it was one of those funny situations where Sales reckoned that I was going to do engineering work, while Engineering said that I was going to help Sales demonstrate the vehicle. Obviously, neither of them wanted to foot the costs! One of the Range Rovers was fitted with air conditioning. It was a system which we were not very proud of, but William Martin-Hurst was quite keen on air conditioning, and he worked with the research people in producing an extremely expensive, very sophisticated system in one of the prototypes. It was so expensive that we never did anything with it.

I did a load of testing around Cape Town and then up around Johannesburg, because of the high altitude there, and we demonstrated to potential customers as

Geof Miller took this Range Rover to South Africa on a combined sales and engineering test, and it is seen here with Table Mountain in the background. The contraption on the roof is an air conditioning system. (Geof Miller)

well as the staff at the manufacturing plant at Cape Town. I took the vehicles out to existing Rover and Land Rover customers all over the place, including a game reserve, where we had a particularly interesting time, although the guy didn't buy any Range Rovers! But the expedition was very worthwhile, in that I was able to prove to the people in South Africa that the vehicles met all the standards that they required in cooling, handling, brakes, and all the rest.

As time went on and things got modified and different markets wanted different specifications, it became something of an ongoing thing that every now and again we had to double check everything we were doing in Britain by going to either a hot or a cold territory to prove things.

Velar's name game, and pre-launch drama

That historically vital Range Rover, the pre-production Velar, is worth commenting on separately, despite everything which has been written about it in the past. Going back to the initial development, we'd had prototype No 1, the 'look-see' vehicle; then No 2 with the correct chassis but wrong body; and No 3, the first to the correct specification. These were followed by 4, 5, 6 and 7, which were all engineering prototypes. Then in late-1969 we built 27 pre-production prototypes. They were assembled on the line with as much tooled material as possible, but with very little trim, and no real seats, but mock-up Land Rover seats instead. We then went on to 20 press cars, which were the NXC series destined to be used for the launch in Cornwall in 1970; this means that anything H-registered was a pre-production Velar, registered prior to the launch. In all there were 47 of them. No production vehicles carried an H plate, and all vehicles built for sale carried J plates.

And it's necessary to put the record straight concerning the name Velar, about which there was a lot of speculation at the time, and still is. Even some people within the company still don't know the true story. The name Velar already existed at the time of the run-up to the Range Rover's launch. The common stories are that it stands for **V**ehicle

Establishment **L**eyland **A**lvis **R**over or **V**8 Engine in **LA**nd **R**over, but the true story is completely different.

There was a little sports car known as the P6 BS, which now sits at the Heritage Museum at Gaydon, which was a joint development between Rover and Alvis, under the link forged between the two organisations before the days of Leyland. Spen King had come up with the design of this two-seater, using the V8 engine, but Alvis had made most of the prototype parts and only one was ever built, by Alvis. The man in charge of it was Mike Dunn, who had been told to create a name for it using a combination of Alvis and Rover letters. It had to be a joint name that could be used on a prototype, and sufficiently obscure to keep the press away from it. Mike had been in engineering for a long time and had done a lot of overseas work and, unlike me, he could speak Italian and Spanish. *Velar*, in Spanish, means 'to watch over', and can be used as 'to keep secret, or quiet'; and *velare* in Italian can mean 'to mist over', 'undercover', or 'veiled'. Using the general sense of the word in these two languages, along with the requirement to use parts of the names of the two companies, he came up with Velar.

With the name established, the sports car was registered as a Velar, by The Velar Motor Company of London. Then, when I needed a name for Range Rovers to be taken out on the road, my car colleague in new vehicle projects said, 'We've registered the little car as a Velar, so why don't you do the same?' So I did, and they were all registered as Velars, and all the tax discs showed them as such. But the subsequent taxing of them created one or two laughs because some simply changed from Velar to Range Rover, some to Land Rover/Range Rover, and one actually became Land Rover/Range Rover/Jeep.

At the time that the launch was approaching I was reporting directly to Peter Wilkes and the date of the great event was being forced on us for late-1969 or perhaps January 1970, but it was far too early and we got an agreement that it would be put back to late-May 1970 for the initial press announcement, followed by the full launch in June. Peter was concerned as to how we were getting on with solving some of the problems which still afflicted the vehicle. At one of our progress meetings he said to me, 'Write a list of all your worries, then split them into two categories, the first one to include the type which could lead to the breakdown of the vehicle, leaving the owner stranded at the side of the road, and in the second category put those

This photograph was taken at the press launch of the Range Rover in Cornwall in 1970. The journalists who drove the cars were amazed at their versatility.

The press demonstration vehicles being filled up at a normally quiet garage in Cornwall on the day of the 1970 launch. (Geof Miller)

problems which might occur and cause annoyance, but not a breakdown.' So I made the two lists of all the things we were concerned about and went back to him. He looked through them and said, 'Yes, OK, I agree with all your points. So you concentrate on all the ones which could lead to a breakdown situation, at the expense of all the others.'

And that was the way the Range Rover was launched.

Duelling with differentials in the Amazon

The Trans Americas Expedition in February 1972 was a thorough check of the overall Range Rover package in the sense that it started in minus 40° in Alaska and went through Panama at plus 30 or so and then finished off at Tierra del Fuego at minus 10 or 15°. I was involved to the extent that we took two left-hand drive Range Rovers off the production line and did all the modifications that were needed, which, to be honest, were mainly creature comfort ones and specific expedition changes, rather than anything fundamental.

We took the back bench seat out and put a Rover P6 seat in for example, because there were only going to be three people in each vehicle, although the front seats remained standard. We put a small roll bar inside, stowage lockers to stop things sliding around, and for stowing spares, food and drink, etc, and installed a safe, water keg and coffee maker, winch equipment, and so on. Apart from that sort of thing, modifications were restricted to little more than adjustments to the bodywork to allow big swamp tyres to be fitted. We prepared the vehicles and trained the Army drivers in some of the

Geof Miller was flown out to join the 1972 Trans Americas Expedition after a succession of differential failures caused by extreme overloading. Here a vehicle is receiving a little help during one of the countless river crossings on the way through the Amazonian rain forest. (Geof Miller)

techniques which might be required, and then they were flown off to Anchorage in Alaska for the start of the trek.

We got drawn into it in an active sense because, only two days out from Anchorage, one vehicle crashed into a container lorry, and we had to send a load of spares out for the vehicle to be rebuilt at Vancouver. They subsequently got through to Panama City, then went into the jungle ... and started to break differentials. That's when I became known as 'Differential Miller'. The main problem was that they got to Panama City, with the vehicles already fully laden, but they then loaded stuff like inflatable boats, outboard motors and all the gear related to jungle travel as opposed to North American road travel. Unfortunately they hadn't taken out all the other gear which was no longer needed. Even the cold weather spares from Alaska were still aboard. although they were now at the Equator.

The vehicles entered the jungle drastically overloaded, and started breaking differentials; unfortunately the additional spares we'd supplied were still on a ship

This drawing was completed specially for this book by Pete Wilford after the author told him that one of the chapters contained details of the way Geof Miller had flown out to help the Army with their differential problems on the Trans Americas Expedition. The drawing shows Geof trying to explain things to the mechanically unsympathetic crew.

WELL IT'S A BIT TECHNICAL MAJOR, BUT THE THINGAMYJIG THAT WHIZZES ROUND & ROUND HAS COME ADRIFT FROM THE FLOPPY LUMP AT ONE END AND ALL THE LITTLE BITS & PIECES HAVE TUMBLED OUT - IN LAYMANS TERMS, YOUR PROP. SHAFT'S KNACKERED !

somewhere in the Atlantic, so we flew them some differentials in. They used these to replace the broken ones and carried on, then started breaking them again. Each time this happened I got a phone call at about 2am from the Ministry of Defence saying they wanted this, that, and the other. In the end they'd used all the differentials and were wondering what to do. We got another of these 2am messages, and I found myself being told to catch the next plane to Panama!

I was flown into the jungle in a US Army helicopter, armed with yet more spare differentials which I fitted, and then I set off with the expedition from the spot where they'd been stuck for a fortnight. We got to a village with an airstrip, where I took everything out of the vehicles and found to my horror just how much they were still carrying which was no longer needed. We had earlier tried driving the Range Rovers down the airstrip and found the bump rubbers were in constant contact with the axles. They were never coming off, so there was no axle movement, because they were so heavily overloaded.

The trek continued with only the absolutely necessary equipment loaded. We'd got a small Beaver aircraft which could do air drops for us, and we could get equipment to the vehicles at every river crossing point, so there was just no need to carry everything in the way they had been doing. Having sorted it out, I then drove with them for three or four weeks. The vehicle that I drove had one differential still in it which had been there when I repaired the others, and this broke, but beyond that the vehicle I drove never broke a differential. And the other one also only broke one more.

We had been concerned that we might have had a quality problem with the differentials, but once I saw what they were doing it was immediately obvious that the drastic overloading was causing the problem. Particularly with the load on the roof, when you got the vehicle on a 30° slope, like when climbing out of a river, the load on the back axle was three times what it should have been, whereas the front axle loading was virtually zero. On top of that they'd got these big swamp tyres which were like four big flywheels, and once you'd got those spinning if they then caught up a bit of traction from something it was like trying to stop a flywheel suddenly, and something had to go, either the half shaft or the differential.

Once the load had been taken out I rearranged the tyres and just put ordinary 750x16 traction tyres on instead of the swamps and modified the driving techniques — using the winches more — and we were straight away out of trouble. We did have more differential breakages, because our transmission chief designer had suggested trying a couple of differentials in which the gear teeth had not been hardened, on the theory that they might not snap off like carrots, but simply bend a bit. But they didn't — they bent and then broke.

It was only the differentials which succumbed to the torture, and not a single half shaft broke. And that's despite the fact that they had been running the vehicles until a rear differential broke, then continued on just the front differential, until this broke. Then they towed the dead one with the good one, until its rear differential broke, and then had to stop with just one good differential between two vehicles. In addition to this, when a differential breaks a gear tooth often

RIGHT *The Range Rover's original design team considered it crucial to give the vehicle excellent off-roading characteristics. The latest version of this superb machine is truly at home in the most difficult surroundings, yet is at the same time the most luxurious and sophisticated vehicle built by Land Rover.* (Nick Dimbleby)

After the Trans Americas Expedition the Range Rovers which made the incredible journey were shipped back to Land Rover. Here Sir George Farmer, Rover's chairman (centre), and managing director A. B. Smith (right) discuss some of the technicalities with expedition member Army Captain G. Thompson. (National Motor Museum)

comes out through the casing like a bullet out of a gun. When this happened they were asking for new axle cases, which was daft because it was costly and time consuming. I changed all this when I got there. If we had a hole in the axle case we just stripped it down, cleaned it all up, tapped a bit of metal into the hole, put Araldite on the inside and outside and carried on.

Here was the British Army, supposed to be saving us in times of war, and they couldn't even keep a vehicle on the road. If they bent a track rod they chucked it away and requested a replacement. If I bent a track rod I'd just straighten it on the same stump I bent it on! Eventually, after repeating this about three times, it would become so weak you'd have to throw it away, but certainly not every time.

Chapter Six

Camel Trophy, the ultimate test

Land Rovers are put to the test every day by their users, and with an extraordinarily high proportion of them being used in the rough and tumble of agriculture and construction, the daily round of the average Land Rover is tough in the extreme. Yet there's one annual test for Solihull machinery which overshadows even the most arduous everyday workout: the Camel Trophy.

Typically, the Camel Trophy is a hard slog lasting several weeks through the most inhospitable countryside imaginable. It may be through desert, jungle, or mountains, or quite often all three, and is always an extreme challenge. The nature of the event has changed considerably over the years, along with what the competi-

Land Rover makes an enormous contribution towards the Camel Trophy in providing all the specially-prepared vehicles. However, the event is a superb showcase! (National Motor Museum)

tion expects of the people involved. Yet one aspect remains constant: the vehicles all carry the Land Rover badge, and they'll be facing the most intensive and demanding challenges imaginable, testing their mechanical reliability, build quality, and even the very basis of their design, to the limit.

The Camel Trophy has been run since 1980, and in every year but one the vehicles have been Land Rovers. The very first Trophy covered 1,600km of the Transamazonica Highway in Brazil; it was a small event by more recent standards, with three teams, all German, driving Jeeps. The following year was again an all-German event, but it marked the start of the use of Land Rover vehicles, with the organisers specifying Range Rovers as the only machinery capable of withstand-ing the challenge. And that's how it has been ever since, with either Range Rovers, Defenders, or Discoverys being chosen for the arduous challenge, apart from 1998, when the newly introduced Freelander was selected. Land Rover Ltd has been associated intimately with the event since 1981, and has been a co-sponsor since 1992. The 1981 event, which took place in the unforgiving equatorial jungles of Sumatra, was a true baptism of fire for the Solihull company and inspired Land Rover to an ever-growing level of involvement which culminated in sponsor-ship.

Contrary to some misconceptions, the Camel Trophy is not a race in the manner of the Paris–Dakar, but a team event in which the abilities of those taking part are put to the test in a variety of ways.

Land Rovers were undertaking expeditions many years before the Camel Trophy. This Series I 86-inch was on the Oxford and Cambridge Far Eastern Expedition in the 1950s, and is seen here on the road from Katmandu in Nepal. (National Motor Museum)

Traditionally it has involved a mixture of driving skills and the ability to come through a series of extremely challenging special tests, such as crossing tropical rivers or coping with normally undriveable desert terrain. But over the years there's been a gradual shift away from this towards a lifestyle approach in which canoeing, mountain biking, and navigation play a major part. What has not changed is that a series of 'good works', such as building schools or clinics, form an integral part of the event. And although care of the environment has always been a major consideration, recent years have seen this become one of the key factors. Its motto of 'leave only footprints and take only photographs' says a lot about the Camel Trophy, and the policy of using only existing tracks and trails ensures that there's no damage to the terrain or any-thing connected with it. Were it not for this, Land Rover would undoubtedly not wish to be connected with the event.

Millions of hopefuls

Interest in the Camel Trophy is quite staggering with, recently, more than nine million people applying to take part. Little wonder, then, that Land Rover sees it as such a valuable promotional exercise that it is prepared to invest very heavily in the provision of vehicles, all of which are specially prepared. The return on this investment is the world-wide exposure the vehicles receive in this prestigious and tough event. General media coverage of the Camel Trophy in Britain is poor, but in many other European countries and elsewhere around the globe it is massive, including major television coverage from

Such is the enthusiasm for Camel Trophy vehicles that there's even a club exclusively for them. Here, Camel Discoverys are on display at a Land Rover show.

the journalists and television crews who are an integral part of the whole circus.

There can be little doubt that the eight years in which the Discovery was the official vehicle, beginning in 1990, has done a lot for Discovery sales. It was particularly important for Land Rover that the world should see the Discovery in really tough conditions, especially in the vehicle's earlier years, because Solihull had to ensure the motoring public were made aware that, beneath the Discovery's attractive skin, was a Land Rover just as durable as any other. In this respect, the Camel Trophy has played an important part in establishing the Discovery as a strong, go-anywhere machine, and there's no doubt that this, in turn, has added to the Land Rover legend in general.

The Discovery has, in fact, been the most popular of all Land Rover's vehicles with Camel Trophy participants, support teams, organisers, and the hundreds of press who are flown in and out for a few days in team cars; only a very select few draw all-the-way tickets. The Discovery's off-roading ability, especially when kitted up with the tall tyres, winch, roll cage, and other equipment which is part and parcel of all Camel machinery, has never been in question with organisers and participants, while the ride comfort and general spaciousness of the cabin have gone down especially well. Making full use of the rear boot area, plus the familiar Camel Trophy roof rack, the Discovery has an amazing load carrying capability. True, it makes the already tall vehicle a little top heavy, but this has not proved a handicap.

As well as the high-profile Camel Trophy, Discoverys have been involved in numerous exciting expeditions. This photograph was taken during the Calvert Centenary Expedition, a five-week trek through the deserts of Western Australia. (National Motor Museum)

The Discovery has been just as popular with the technical support teams, whose job it is to keep things moving in the event of mechanical problems, as it has been with the competitors. The fact that it is an easy vehicle to work on has proved particularly advantageous on the few occasions difficulties have struck on jungle tracks or in inhospitable desert regions. And the adaptability which permits easy conversion into a mobile workshop, communications vehicle, raft-carrier, and medical support car has made it countless friends along Camel Trophy trails.

The Freelander made its Camel Trophy debut in the 1998 event in South America, officially named the Tierra del Fuego Camel Trophy. The 5,000km run down the demanding western side of South America was the longest-ever Trophy, testing the heavily laden Freelanders to the limit. However, the vehicle had already proved itself up to the job by completing a recce trip in 1997, several months before its official launch. Nick Horne, Camel Trophy event director, was most impressed and reported that he had every confidence the Freelander would prove ideal. He tested a five-door petrol-engined version in all the same conditions that would confront the contestants in August 1988. This included driving on some of the highest roads in the world, through arid desert, along mountain tracks, and across glaciers and rivers, and took fully into account the fact that in the southern hemisphere August falls in the winter, and winter in the Andes can pose a severe challenge to anyone in a motor vehicle. Although the Freelander is not designed to be a true off-roader in the

It could be a scene straight out of the Camel Trophy, but it is actually a quarry near Stamford, Lincolnshire, and the Discovery is being used for off-road driver training for Voluntary Service Overseas personnel.

manner of the Defender, Discovery, and Range Rover, it is, in fact, adequately competent off the tarmac. Nick finished his trip very impressed, and perhaps just a little surprised, that the vehicle had done so well.

In the event itself each team's Freelander was teamed up with a Defender 110 as a support vehicle, carrying the additional equipment that now forms part of the Camel Trophy, including bicycles and inflatable boats, as well as full recovery gear. For the Freelander's Camel Trophy introduction a special 'outfitting' session was underway at the factory long before the event. Nick Berry of the Special Vehicle Operations section had the job of organising and fitting the special equipment, just as he had done before with Discoverys and Defenders. As with these previous Trophy Land Rovers, the Freelanders were fitted with a full roll cage, bull bar, and roof-mounted lights for this most demanding of all events. In addition the suspension was strengthened, with higher rate springs and tougher shock absorbers to cope with the combination of heavy loads and cross-country operation.

There's no doubt that the Camel Trophy has now begun to do for the Freelander what it did for the Discovery through its long-term, and very enviable, choice as official vehicle. Quite simply, there is no better showcase ... as Land Rover fully realises.

Changing face of the Trophy

The Camel Trophy has now moved away from the test of endurance, toughness and Indiana Jones style adventure with which it established itself, to become an adventurous lifestyle journey in which resourcefulness, and concern for the environment and the people living in remote areas, are of prime importance. To a degree, sporting activities now play a more important part than the one-time crucial ability to get a vehicle through seemingly impossible conditions. Indeed, there wasn't one part of the 1998 event which was not held on roads or tracks clearly shown on local maps — although some of the tracks were nothing more than rocky pathways which, especially in winter, are often extremely difficult, if not impossible, in any vehicle less capable than a Freelander. The change has come about partly through the natural evolution of the event, partly because of changing attitudes, and partly because of the very different nature of the Freelander, which was designed as a general recreational car with a more youthful appeal than previous Solihull vehicles.

The 1998 Tierra del Fuego expedition introduced, for the first time, the freedom for teams to choose their own routes on the run southwards, plus their own challenges. This tactical free thinking challenged the teams somewhat more, in that they were, to an extent, creating their own event, rather than simply going where everybody else did. Teams collected points by choosing a series of specific competition locations to visit along their chosen route. The points scored depended on the difficulty of reaching the location and the mix of activities required to overcome the chosen challenge. These activities included kayaking, mountain biking and, of course, 4×4 driving, plus others more specific to the winter conditions of South America's mountain regions, such as skiing, snow boarding, and snow shoeing.

But as well as the individual team challenges there were opportunities for the teams to work together and explore together in non-competitive situations. Spread out along the route were three meeting points where the teams were able to gather to swap experiences. Each of the meeting points was chosen for its stunning location and potential for adventure.

Perhaps the most outstanding of these was at Futaleufu where, for those with the courage, there was the opportunity to white-water raft down one of the fastest and most exciting rivers anywhere in the world. The others were at Pucon, with a 2,800m (9,185ft) snow-covered volcano proving irresistible to climbers, and Torres del Paine, with ice-climbing across a stunning glacier.

The route facing the Freelanders and their teams from 20 countries was a fraction under 5,000km (3,100 miles) and was one of the most interesting in the event's history. The starting point was Santiago, the capital of Chile, which stands at the foot of the Andes and is one of the major centres of the Patagonia region, which comprises Argentina and Chile. From there the convoy moved ever southwards, heading eventually for Ushuaia, which is the southernmost point of the world accessible by road and the capital of the province of Tierra del Fuego, settled originally by Scots, despite its Spanish name.

Organisational nightmare

Only when you look at the full history of the Camel Trophy do you realise just how tough it has been over the years, frequently visiting places where vehicles are rarely seen, and travelling through the world's most isolated, beautiful, and least visited locations.

In many ways the real heroes are the organisers, with Nick Horne and his teams having to deal with everything from obtaining permission from governments to air-lifting groups of journalists to the middle of nowhere for their stints on the event. Planning commences a couple of years ahead, gets pretty intense during the incredible process of selection and the shipment of team vehicles and support machines, and then is put to its ultimate

Participation in the Camel Trophy helped convince people that the Discovery was capable of tackling difficult off-road situations. Here the author copes with deep, rutted mud in an ex-Camel Trophy machine.

test each year during the event itself. And, of course, the vehicles all have to be shipped back again. Land Rover's involvement is also intense, and involves committing an appropriate number of chosen vehicles to production, followed by their preparation, which involves countless hours installing all the special equipment.

It is not often that Camel Trophy drivers have to face conditions like these, in which a Freelander is battling with deep snow in the 1998 event. Steamy jungles and arid deserts are the normal fare for this toughest of challenges. (Carl Rodgerson)

The event promotes Land Rover and Camel Trophy adventure clothing and equipment, the original link with cigarettes having faded into the background over recent years.

Camel Trophy routes and winners

The history of the Camel Trophy from 1980 to 1997 reads like a world-wide travelogue, and apart from the first year, the single constant factor has been Land Rover's involvement (distances are given where available):

1980 Transamazonica
Transamazonica Highway, Balem to Santarem (1,600km/994 miles); vehicle, Jeep; winners, Klaus Karthna-Dircks/Uwe Machel (Germany).

1981 Sumatra
Medan to Jambi (1,600km/994 miles); vehicle, Range Rover; winners, Christian Swobada/Knuth Mentel (Germany).

1982 Papua New Guinea
Mont Hagen to Madang; vehicle, Range Rover; winners, Cesare Geraudo/Giuliaro Giongol (Italy). Special tests were introduced to the Camel Trophy in this event. The extreme conditions by day and night were a severe test, and progress was slowed by fast-moving rapids with many nights spent building bridges.

1983 Zaire
Kinshasa to Kinsangani (1,600km/994 miles); vehicle, Land Rover SIII 88-inch; winners, Henk Bont and Frans Hey (Holland). The first event in Africa, with terrain ranging from knee-deep mud to desert sand and temperatures above 45°C at times.

1984 Brazil
Transamazonica Highway, Santarem to Manaus; vehicle, Land Rover 110; winners, Maurizio Lavi and Alfredo Redaelli (Italy). A particularly severe rainy season made it impossible to drive the original route, but the alternative proved little easier with virtually non-stop mud.

1985 Borneo
Samarinda to Balikpapan; vehicle, Land Rover 90; winner, Heinz Kallin/Bernd Strohdach (Germany); Team Spirit award, Carlos Probst/Tito Rosenberg (Brazil). The Team Spirit award was introduced for this event, which, because of severe rain and swollen rivers, progressed very slowly through unexplored territory in Indonesian Borneo. Some days saw only 2–3km (1.2–1.8 miles) covered, and stranded vehicles had to be airlifted by helicopter.

1986 Australia
Cooktown to Darwin (3,218km/2,000 miles); vehicle, Land Rover 90; winner Jacques Mambre/Michel Courvallet (France); Team Spirit award, Glenn Jones/Ronn Begg (Australia). Fast progress was made through the dry and dusty outback, averaging 247km (154 miles) each day. Raft-building led to a 24-hour delay at one river crossing.

1987 Madagascar
Diego Suarez to Fort Dauphin (2,252km/1,400 miles); vehicle, Range Rover TD; winners, Mauro Miele/ Vincenzo Tota (Italy); Team Spirit award, Jaime Puig/Victor Muntane (Spain). The convoy chalked up the first north to south motoring journey in Madagascar's history, running from tropical rain forest to arid savannah.

1988 Sulawesi
Manado to Ujang Padang (2,092km/1,300 miles); vehicle, Land Rover 110; winners, Galip Gurel/Ali Deveci (Turkey); Team Spirit award, Jim Benson/Marc Day (UK). Two series of special tasks were introduced for this event, and bridge-building and route repairs occupied much time on the drive across the mountains and dense jungle trails.

1989 The Amazon
Alta Floresta to Manaus (1,600km/994 miles); vehicle, Land Rover 110; winners, Bob Ives/Joe Ives (UK); Team Spirit award, Frank Dewitte/Peter Denys (Belgium). Returning to the Amazon jungle for the tenth anniversary, this was probably the most demanding of all Camel Trophy events.

1990 Siberia
Bratsk to Irkutsk; vehicle, Discovery Tdi 3-door; winners, Rob Kamps/Stijn Luykx (Holland); Team Spirit award, Carlos Berreto/Fernando Martin (Canary Islands). In a Camel Trophy which was far removed

Parading for the camera before being shipped off to the 1991 event are the 36 vehicles, all Discoverys apart from some support Defenders, also supplied by Land Rover. The Camel Trophy helped establish the Discovery as a tough off-roader, which is why Land Rover was keen to supply these vehicles from the outset. (National Motor Museum)

from the more normal jungle terrain, this was the first international motor sport event to be held in the Soviet Union.

1991 Tanzania–Burundi
Dar es Salaam to Bujumbura (1,600km/994 miles); vehicle, Discovery Tdi 5-door; winners and Team Spirit award, Menderes Utku/Bulent Ozler (Turkey); Special Tasks award, Joseph Altmann/Peter Widhalm (Austria). This was the first time the event had crossed two countries, retracing Livingstone's trail to the source of the Nile.

1992 Guyana
Manaus, Brazil, to Georgetown, Guyana (1,600km/994 miles); vehicle, Discovery Tdi 5-door; winners, Alwin Arnold/Urs

Bruggisser (Switzerland); Team Spirit award, Dan Amon/Jim West (USA); Special Tasks award, Eric Cassaigne/Patrick Lafabrie (France).

1993 Sabah–Malaysia
Circumnavigation from Kota Kinabalu (1,500km/932 miles); vehicle, Discovery Tdi 5-door; winners, Tim Hensley/Mike Hussey (USA); Team Spirit award, Ellis Martin/Francisco Zarate (Canary Islands); Special Tasks award, Paul Gasser/Loup Tournand (France). During this event participants built an ecological field monitoring station in an unexplored jungle area known locally as The Lost World.

1994 Argentina, Paraguay and Chile
Iguazo Falls to Hornitos (2,500km/1,554

miles); vehicle, Discovery Tdi 5-door; winners and Special Tasks award, Carlos Martinez/Jorge Corella (Spain); Team Spirit award, Klaus Albert Hass/Etienne van Eeden (South Africa). Covering three countries for the first time, the convoy experienced the most diverse climatic conditions – extremely severe at times – yet seen in a Camel Trophy event.

1995 Mundo Maya

Lamanai, Belize, through Mexico, Guatemala, El Salvador, and Honduras, to Xunantunich, Belize (1,700km/1,057 miles); vehicle, Discovery Tdi 5-door; winners and Special Tasks award, Zdenek Nemec/Marek Rocejdl (Czech Republic); Team Spirit award, Pavel Bogomolov/

Sergei Fenev (Russia). The event provided a unique insight into one of the western hemisphere's greatest civilisations, the Maya, along with an unsurpassed mixture of challenges and adventure.

1996 Kalimantan

Balikpapan to Pontianak (1,850km/1,150 miles); vehicle, Discovery Tdi 5-door; winners and Land Rover award, Miltos Farmakis and Nikos Sotirchos (Greece); Team Spirit award, Samuel de Beer/Pieter du Plessis (South Africa); Special Tasks award, Dmitriy Surin/Alexi Svirkov (Russia). In many ways this was the most arduous Trophy so far, with heat, monsoon rains, and dreadful mud causing great problems. In one six-day

Typical action from the Camel Trophy as competitors on the 1996 event in Kalimantan negotiate a dangerous ravine crossing after constructing the bridge themselves. (National Motor Museum)

Although Camel Trophy drivers obviously try to avoid situations like this, they are not always successful. This support Defender in the 1996 event slid over the edge of a nasty drop, and required careful recovery. (Nick Dimbleby)

period contestants covered only 50km (31 miles).

1997 Mongolia

Circular route from Ulaanbaatar (1,835km/1,140 miles); vehicle, Discovery 5-door; winners, Stefan Auer/ Albrecht Thausing (Austria); Team Spirit award, Rikard Backman/Marie Hensen (Sweden). The extremes of Mongolia's climate, from minus 10° to a sweltering 40°, along with terrain ranging from the barren wastelands of the Gobi Desert to dense mountain forests, made this yet another outstanding Camel Trophy.

Chapter Seven

The unbeatable Defender

There is no other general-purpose or utility vehicle anywhere in the world with the off-roading capability of the Land Rover Defender. In its short wheelbase form it is an unrivalled workhorse wherever toughness and versatility are called for, and in the hands of enthusiasts it is the world's greatest off-roader. And

No other vehicle has the off-roading capability of the Defender 90, which makes off-roading both safe and enjoyable.

standing proudly alongside the 90 is its slightly older sibling, the long wheelbase 110, which has immense load-carrying capacity, is one of the world's most versatile people carriers, and is also a great off-roader.

Yet despite this global supremacy, there was nothing revolutionary about the first member of this great family, the One Ten (as it was known initially), when it first appeared on the world's stage in 1983. Land Rover just don't do things that way — or at least, they didn't then. Furthermore, the Ninety evolved from the One Ten, rather than the two vehicles entering the world with a big bang and a joint launch. It took 35 years for the working Land Rover to develop from its

original design into the superb machine that was the One Ten. And yet in many respects the One Ten did not evolve from its Series III predecessor; only in its body styling and some of the interior fitments could it be said to enjoy a close relationship with the 109-inch model which had gone before. To be more accurate, the One Ten evolved partly from the Series III Stage 1 V8 109, and partly from the Range Rover, which, at the time of the new model's introduction, was already 13 years old.

Perhaps the most important thing about the One Ten was that it looked like a Land Rover, a fact of crucial importance to Land Rover customers around the world, and an area where the company

The first utility Land Rover to be fitted with coil springs was the One Ten, launched in 1983. It led to the Ninety a year later. (National Motor Museum)

had been especially clever in the development of this long-overdue new model. But although the One Ten was very much in the mould of the utility vehicles of the past, this new Land Rover was in essence a Range Rover with a longer chassis and a modified Series III body.

The transformation of everything but the body and interior of the luxury 4×4 estate car into a new, but recognisable, Land Rover utility vehicle was, in the world of motor manufacturing, an unbelievably simple way of producing what was seen generally as a revolutionary new Land Rover. The single most surprising fact is that it had taken all those years from the launch of the Range Rover to do it. Yet Rover had very good reasons for doing it that way, among them the key matters of customer confidence, product familiarity, and very limited finance for new models.

Yet, notwithstanding all that, given the relative simplicity of the job of turning a Range Rover into a Land Rover, it is even more surprising when looking back from today's perspective, that the job seems to have been done in two rather laborious stages, starting with the 109-inch Series III being given the Range Rover engine and transmission to become the Stage 1, seen for the first time in public at the Geneva Motor Show in March 1979. However, there were very good reasons for this, mostly to do with cash, and the Stage 1 was a rapid response to Stage 1 of the Government's expansion of Land Rover – whence the name of this vehicle, which was the first step towards the all-new Land Rover which the company then began working on in earnest.

The Stage 1 proved a number of points for Land Rover, most important of these being confirmation that a powerful, more civilised Land Rover was demanded, not only by farmers and the like, but also by the then fast-growing number of people who wanted a good 4×4 vehicle for everyday and recreational use. The Range Rover was popular, yes, but there was ever more demand for a better Land Rover. By now the Series III was an extremely old-fashioned machine, hopelessly outclassed in just about every way.

The One Ten makes its entrance

So along came the One Ten, and what a reception it received. The new Land Rover took the Stage 1 concept a lot further, although it used Series III bodywork with only a few modifications. Added to the Range Rover engine and transmission were the Range Rover's coil springs, but there were variations on this most attractive theme; you could also specify a 2.3-litre (as the familiar 2,286cc unit was now called by many people) petrol or diesel engine, both with five-speed gearbox, whereas with the V8 you got only four gears, as on the Range Rover. But the machine to go for was the V8, regardless of its four-speed gearbox and astonishing thirst, which normally worked out to about 11mpg when working very hard and a very best of about 15mpg. Most noticeable styling change from the Series III – which continued to be produced alongside the new model – was the introduction of a one-piece windscreen, along with deformable wheelarch extensions and a revised grille. There were still horizontally sliding windows for the front doors, though.

The coil spring suspension gave significantly better axle articulation, a fact to which all Series III owners will readily testify; the new vehicle's front wheel movement was 50 per cent better than the leaf sprung model's, while there was 25 per cent more at the rear. And because the rear axle was mounted 3in (76mm) closer to the rear of the chassis than on the Range Rover, the reduced rear overhang improved the departure angle considerably – always a problem when off-roading a Range Rover. Unfortunately, only the V8 offered sensible road-going performance. The four-cylinder petrol engine's power output was a meagre 74bhp against the V8's 114bhp. The diesel was even worse, of course, with only 60bhp.

At the time 70 per cent of Land Rover sales around the world were long wheelbase models, so it is not difficult to see why the One Ten was the first of the new machines to arrive. The company invested £7 million in its chassis plant, which incorporated 16 welding robots programmed to make more than 400 separate welds to each chassis. This was Land Rover's first use of robots, installed for improved consistency and quality as well as faster production.

The chassis was described at the time as being notably sturdier than the Range Rover's already very strong frame on which it was based, swelling to a depth of more than 7.5in (190mm) at the centre. The chassis was given four new jacking points, at each end of the longitudinal members, and the fuel tank was sited for maximum protection. The County Station Wagon was fitted as standard with a Boge Hydromat self-levelling unit, important to retain full rear spring movement when heavily loaded, which was optional on all other variants. The Land Rover front beam axle was located by forged steel leading radius arms and a Panhard rod. The Salisbury rear axle had tubular trailing links controlling fore and aft movement and an A-frame to limit lateral movement. County versions were given a rear anti-roll bar as well.

The servo assisted brakes used 11.8-inch discs at the front, a departure for Land Rovers, although Range Rovers were, of course, disc-braked. The turning circle was improved by all of 5ft (1.5m)

The 90 County Station Wagon combines the toughness and go-anywhere capability of all 90s with car-like comforts, making it a supremely versatile machine.

compared with the 109, partly because of the change of springing, but also due to the wider track. Power assistance was offered as an option, very welcome for a working Land Rover. The four cylinder models were given a strengthened version of the LT77 gearbox, developed originally for the Rover SD1 and then Jaguars, but even with additional strength this was not up to the torque of the V8. The V8 version was therefore given the LT95 gearbox used in the Range Rover and Series III. The lack of a high fifth ratio for main road cruising was to a small degree compensated for by the availability of a Fairey overdrive as an aftermarket fitment. Something not always appreciated these days is that four-cylinder customers could specify the familiar selectable two-wheel drive transmission and freewheeling hubs if they wanted an alternative to the permanent four wheel drive system.

Autocar took a One Ten on an extended test drive around Scotland early in 1983, including an off-road stint on Skye and the full length of General Wade's military road over the mountains from the southern end of Loch Ness. The magazine was enormously impressed with the new Land Rover, both with its performance on all types of surfaced road and with its much improved off-roading ability. Land Rover had at last made the breakthrough many of its customers had been waiting for. But had they? What about the short wheelbase model?

Enter the Ninety

It wasn't until the following year that the Ninety was introduced. In most respects it was a shortened version of the One Ten,

The vehicle on the right is Ninety prototype number 2, with a cut-down One Ten chassis. This was the first to have the 90.9-inch wheelbase of the production Ninety. It is photographed here alongside the experimental Series III fitted with the Rover P6 car engine. Both vehicles are part of the Dunsfold Collection and have been driven extensively by the author.

as a close examination of prototype No 2 in the Dunsfold Collection in Surrey will rapidly demonstrate. On this vehicle, which was the first to have the production wheelbase length of 90.9in, it can clearly be seen how the development exercise had proceeded. The cuts and joins on the chassis are proof that it was built on a cut-down One Ten frame, while the way the 88-inch rear body was extended for this second pre-production truck is there for all to see.

There was no V8 option, just the same two four-cylinder engines as on the One Ten. And, with hardly anybody wanting the two-wheel drive option on the One Ten (there's a surprise!), this choice was sensibly dropped on the Ninety. Another change was the replacement of the Salisbury rear axle used on the One Ten by one of Land Rover's own. And, at last, there were wind-up windows, introduced also on the One Ten with the launch of the Ninety.

Early in 1985 the Ninety's missing ingredient, the V8, joined the line-up, transforming an already excellent machine into one with a level of all-round ability hitherto only dreamed of. Moreover, the engine was mated to the new LT85 five-speed gearbox already being used in the Range Rover. Made in Spain by Santana, and using mainly Santana components, the new gearbox gave the V8 Ninety wonderful road-going performance, as it did the One Ten on which it was also offered.

Everybody who drove the Ninety V8 raved about it, and I was one of them. The press were invited to play around with them towards the end of April 1985, and I well remember my own first impressions. At the time I was the publisher of *Motor*, running an early five-speed Range Rover as a long-term test car, and I just couldn't believe how much the engine and gearbox combination I was used to on an everyday basis had improved the short wheelbase Land Rover.

Much as I loved my Range Rover, I would willingly have swapped it for the Ninety V8.

There's nowhere in the world that Defenders haven't been! These two Spanish-registered 90s were photographed in North Africa during an event sponsored by Warn. (Vince Cobley).

Four-cylinder versions of the One Ten and Ninety became somewhat better with a capacity increase to 2.5 litres; they were beginning to get towards the level of power they needed. With the capacity increase the diesel's power went from 60 to 67bhp, which was enough to get the Ninety up to 68mph (109kph), eventually, if conditions were favourable. Perhaps more importantly, the extra power and torque improved the diesel's off-roading usefulness.

But it was not until the end of 1986 that the big leap forward was made with the diesel unit when, after two years of development, it was modified to take a Garrett AiResearch T2 turbocharger, lifting the power to 85bhp at 4,000rpm, and the all-important torque to 150lb/ft at 1,800rpm. Changes to the engine from the normally aspirated 2.5-litre diesel were substantial. A new block, with integral turbocharger oil feed and drain, was developed, along with a revised crankshaft with improved bearing lubrication, new pistons and rings, and nimonic exhaust valves. Injection was by a DPS self-priming pump, and a new lightweight starter motor, with higher cranking speed, was introduced. The cooling system was uprated with an improved viscous fan and an oil cooler as standard to cope with the extra heat.

Road performance was much improved, with a top speed of 76mph (122kph), and at last the diesel Land Rover could tow a trailer, horse-box, or caravan without struggling desperately for breath. But given the popularity of the Ninety as an off-road worker and, by now, as a recreational machine, the extra power from the diesel was perhaps even more useful on the rough stuff.

Defender's the name

The second-stage Land Rover family which had begun with the One Ten in 1983 finally came of age in the 1991 model year. Amid not a little controversy the utility Land Rovers were given a name for the first time – Defender. With the company's vehicle range having expanded in 1989 with the Discovery it was felt that everything should now be called something specific, rather than be known by its wheelbase length, which had been the case since 1948. Unfortunately the choice of Defender was seen as too military and aggressive by many commentators and private individuals; but the heat died down after a while.

Much more important was the adoption from the Discovery of the company's first direct injection, turbocharged, intercooled diesel engine, the 200 Tdi. This engine had proved exceptionally popular with the Discovery, and was scheduled for the revamped utility models for their introduction in Defender guise in 1990. It was to prove the most important thing to happen to the 90 and 110 since their inception. Quite simply, it was a superb engine which advanced Land Rover's reputation as engine makers by leaps and bounds. The Tdi had the same dimensions as the then current turbo diesel and was based around it, but it was essentially a totally new engine, with specially developed block, pistons, con-rods, and alloy head, although it retained the earlier unit's crankshaft.

The engine was pushed ahead within Land Rover, despite a lot of pressure on the company to buy in an engine rather than producing its own. Fortunately for the hundreds of thousands of satisfied drivers who have subsequently used the 200 Tdi and the follow-up 300 Tdi in Discoverys, Range Rovers, and Defenders, the decision was made to stick with it – but it was a close-run thing, and the final go-ahead only came nine months before the Discovery's launch.

The 130 Crew Cab is a particularly useful vehicle for organisations which require off-road mobility for several people plus a payload.

The Tdi was put into the Defender in a very slightly different state of tune, giving 107bhp instead of 111bhp, and a flatter torque curve, with 188lb/ft at 1,800rpm rather than the Discovery's 192lb/ft at the same engine speed. However, these figures represent 26 per cent more power and 25 per cent more torque than the turbo diesel and, because of the unit's much improved efficiency, 25 per cent better fuel economy. Other improvements at the same time included better seats, a little more elbow room, and even a courtesy light, offered for the first time as a standard fitment in a working Land Rover.

The V8 engine remained the alternative choice to the new diesel, but was now far less attractive to most users because the Tdi gave nearly as much power, and the same level of torque, as the 3.5-litre petrol engine. Alongside this was the fact that, with care, it was now possible to get a consumption figure of 30mpg, whereas there can be few V8 90 or 110 owners who have ever bettered 20mpg. To go half as far again on a tank of fuel while travelling at the same speed is quite a selling point.

With the Tdi gaining admirers rapidly, the V8 began to lose ground, and in 1995 Land Rover began phasing out the V8 powered Defenders for the home market, so that the Tdi became the only engine

One of the most desirable versions of the Defender 90 is the North American Specification model, with V8 engine. This one even has an appropriate registration.

option, other than in North America and a few other export destinations where diesel power had never proved popular. North Americans, however, were being treated particularly well when they bought Defenders, because not only did they have a V8 option, but this had been in 3.9-litre form since 1993, the year they had also been offered the extremely attractive soft-top 90 with its distinctive heavy roll cage.

Although the Defender has been steadily updated, another milestone was the introduction of the revised 300 Tdi engine in 1994. The unit had required updating to keep ahead of new noise and emission standards, and although the power charac-teristics changed slightly with even higher levels, the new engine remained reassuringly familiar to its users. It was fitted to the Discovery and Range Rover Classic as well as the Defender, and in all options was given the much improved R380 five-speed gearbox.

At the time of writing there was much discussion about the Defender replacement, and whether Land Rover would opt for dramatic changes or preferably, in the view of most users, simply update and civilise the existing machine even more. Informed opinion suggests that the familiar and highly practical shape will remain essentially unchanged, with a new engine, and, eventually more use of plastics and

Two Defenders (a 110 and 130) and a Discovery were the official support vehicles for the Paris–Moscow–Beijing Marathon Raid. (National Motor Museum)

LEFT Happy faces all round as the Solihull factory celebrates the 1,500,000th Defender to leave the production line. (National Motor Museum)

advanced electronics. The one thing there is no doubt about is that, even if it is given a new name, the Defender will continue in one form or another for a very long time to come.

And that will be wonderful!

Chapter Eight

The mighty V8

The Rover V8 is one of the world's most significant engines. It has enjoyed a degree of success which is only rivalled in Britain by three other great power units – the legendary Jaguar XK, and the 'working class' A-series and B-

The Range Rover was Rover's third vehicle to use the V8, after the P5 and P6 cars. This publicity shot was taken before the vehicle's launch, which took place before all the engine climate testing work had been completed. The V8 was one of the key reasons for the Range Rover's success. (National Motor Museum)

series duo from BMC. Each of these engines has played a major role in the success of class-leading British cars, and all will go down in history as major players in motor manufacturing. Yet the V8, which is in itself a rare configuration among British engines, came to Rover by a lucky chance after being discarded by the American industry for which it had originally been designed.

The importance of the Rover V8 cannot be underestimated, because without it there is every reason to suggest that the Range Rover would not have been the world-beating success it was, and without the Range Rover the story of Land Rover would have been very different and, at times, far less fruitful. Indeed, without the success of the Range Rover it is possible that Land Rover might not have survived some of its more troublesome times.

As well as being the ideal engine for the Range Rover, the V8 proved to be important for the P5 saloon and crucial to the success of the P6. It enhanced the appeal of the MGB GT, and thereby prolonged its life, and has been retro-fitted to count-

The Rover V8 as fitted to the P6 car. This publicity photograph from the late-1960s was taken before the development work on the Range Rover version of the engine had been completed. (National Motor Museum)

less MGBs and GTs, and has been seen for many years as a replacement for the far less satisfactory Triumph V8 fitted to the Stag. In Land Rover guise it gave the Range Rover the power, character, towing and off-roading ability it otherwise would not have had. No other engine suited the Range Rover so well and, given the thinking which prevailed at Rover at the time, along with cash constraints, it is not at all unreasonable to surmise that an engine of equivalent ability and suitability would never have been designed from scratch.

The success of the Range Rover was crucial to the establishment of sufficient Government confidence in Land Rover for it to be floated as a separate company under the Ryder recommendations of 1978. This, in turn, led to the first-ever 'official' V8 Land Rover, the Stage 1 109-inch, which in turn, and along with the Range Rover, led to the 110, or One Ten as it was known to start with. And from the One Ten came the Ninety, the two machines together forming a family of utility and recreational vehicles, later to be known as Defender 110 and 90, which are so competent that rival manufacturers don't even attempt to compete. Furthermore, the engine which did so much in the early days to establish the

Posing with a Range Rover are the test drivers who clocked up the miles to prove V8s and other engines. Between them they have covered four million miles of test driving. From left to right they are Ron Biddle, Ken Lindsay, Charlie Robbins, Cyril Wheeler, Ray Grundy, and Jim Hadgkiss. (National Motor Museum)

reputation of the One Ten and Ninety was – that's right – the ex-Buick V8. The V8 went into the One Ten from the outset and then, in 1985, a year after its launch, into the Ninety. In the One Ten the 4-speed 3.5-litre V8 was superb, although extremely thirsty. But the transformation over the 4-cylinder 109-inch vehicle it replaced was astonishing. The V8 had earlier provided sufficient power, at last, for the 101 Forward Control, much to the satisfaction of countless military users. And at least they didn't have to pay for the petrol!

In 1989 the V8 grew from the 3.5 litres it had always been to 3.9 litres, and went into the Range Rover in this form, further improving this already legendary machine. It was also used (but still as a 3.5) in the Discovery, right from the beginning of production that year; to drive a V8 Discovery is to appreciate the vehicle at its very best. It is excellent with the diesel engine, yet is transformed with the V8, with a level of refinement and performance which has to be experienced to be believed. Unfortunately, as in all applications, it is also rather thirsty.

The V8 was fully redesigned for the launch of the new Range Rover in 1994, right down to new blocks and heads, all internals, and management system. The new 4.0 version is very, very impressive when compared with everything which has gone before, while the 4.6 is simply out of this world. But, as with the original Range Rover in 1970, the new Range Rover launched a quarter of a century later still relies on an engine which began life in its original form only 15 years after the end of the Second World War. For world-leading vehicles, with levels of luxury, power, sophistication and prestige which are without equal, to be powered by engines which go back that far is astonishing, and a massive endorsement of the quality of design of the original unit.

The latest incarnation is, quite simply, just about the best engine around despite its long lineage and, in both 4.0 and 4.6 forms, it plays a most significant role in this truly outstanding vehicle. It is difficult to imagine anybody being able to come up with an engine more suited to the job. So much so that you can't help wondering what on earth the Americans, who led automotive design and technology from the 1920s to the early-1960s, could have been thinking of when they decided that this particular V8 no longer suited their purposes.

Fireball of the late-1950s

In fact, it is not as simple as that. From about 1955 the American motor industry was putting a great deal of effort into engine development, with considerable emphasis on producing acceptable levels of power from smaller units than they had been accustomed to. Large engines were to remain dominant for some time, but there was considerable pressure to come up with better efficiency and, eventually, smaller engines. The V8 configuration reigned supreme, of course, with the US market happily wedded to its advantages of compact dimensions, healthy power capability, and in-built smoothness and toughness. Against this background, in the second half of the 1950s Buick engineers, as part of General Motors' engine development programme, made a breakthrough when they came up with an economical method of producing an all-aluminium engine.

As a result development work on an all-new, all-alloy V8 gathered pace in the late-1950s and the resulting engine was introduced in 1960 as the Fireball V8, a surprisingly compact, quite revolutionary 3,531cc engine weighing only 360lb. It was so good that General Motors decided it should be fitted as standard to the current Buick range, and as an option in the Pontiac Tempest. In slightly modified form, and renamed Rockette, it was also optional for the Oldsmobile F85.

The engine was an outstanding success, and showed such exceptional competition potential that leading tuners and racing organisations quickly set to work on it. One version, running on alcohol, was turning out a staggering 370 bhp, while another powered the car driven by Dan Gurney in the 1962 Indy 500. Among others who fell under the spell of the Fireball V8 was Bruce McLaren, who created the first Can-Am car when he fitted the engine to the Zerex Special after he bought the car from its original builder, Roger Penske. Yet another big name who realised the V8's potential was Jack Brabham, who, with Repco, produced a single overhead camshaft version for the 1966 Formula 1 grand prix season, and in so doing took his third world title.

Yet despite all this the engine lasted only three years as a General Motors production unit. American motorists, accustomed to cast iron engines, never quite got the hang of using coolant containing the correct solution of corrosion inhibitor throughout the year, leading to corrosion problems. More significantly, the same development work which had given the world this great engine, came up with thin-wall cast iron engines which were much less expensive to manufacture; practically overnight, alloy engines, even those as good as the Fireball, were deemed fit only for the scrap-yard because of the economics of engine production.

Shopping trip to the USA

Rover, meanwhile, was behaving in typical fashion; on the one hand it was sticking

The engine bay of the 88-inch Land Rover used by Geof Miller during development work on the V8 immediately after the manufacturing rights had been bought from Buick. The engine runs well and sounds very healthy, despite all its hard work over many years. This vehicle is in the Dunsfold Collection.

doggedly to the traditional, old-fashioned, high quality which had served it so well in the past, and on the other it was conducting very serious studies into the feasibility of gas turbine, aircraft-type, engines. Rover's engines were far from cutting-edge technology; in the Land Rover division of the company, the mainstay 2.25-litre petrol and diesel engines were extremely good workhorse units and very reliable, but they were considerably lacking in power, and would not have been at all suitable for any serious future development.

Then, in 1962, Rover's recently appointed managing director William Martin-Hurst had a meeting with J. Bruce McWilliams, an American who had been despatched to Europe by the Studebaker-Mercedes sales operation to try to find extra strings for his company's bow. The upshot was that McWilliams later left Studebaker and joined Rover to head up the Solihull company's US sales arm. One of his first recommendations was that Martin-Hurst's people should commence a search for new, more powerful engines in order to give their vehicles better sales potential in America. This was to prove crucial, because it led to Martin-Hurst embarking in January 1964 on a business trip to the USA, where he hoped to find a suitable V8 for which Rover might be able to acquire manufacturing rights.

Purely by chance, while on his way to a meeting with Chrysler he spotted a Fireball V8 in the Wisconsin offices of Mercury Marine where he had gone to talk about gas turbines. Mercury's Karl Kiekhaefer had removed the engine from a Buick sedan with the intention of transplanting it into a speed boat. Martin-Hurst, something of a fireball himself, did some quick checks and established that the engine would fit into a Land Rover, the now ageing P5, and the P6 saloon, which

Many owners fitted V8s to their own Land Rovers before the factory got round to it, and some have fitted them as part of exotic conversions, such as this V8 6x6 based on a Series III.

had only recently been introduced. There and then he somehow persuaded Mercury to ship the engine over to Solihull, and set about the daunting task of trying to get General Motors to sell him the rights to this engine, which they were in the process of discarding anyway.

It took a couple of trips to GM to get negotiations under way, but by summer 1964 things were moving in the direction Martin-Hurst wanted. However, this hadn't been the case back in Solihull, because the idea of using a foreign engine, and an American V8 at that, didn't go down too well with Rover's traditionalists when the engine was removed from its packing case shortly after arriving from Mercury Marine.

Resistance at Rover

Before the purchase talks could commence, or were even arranged, there was strong resistance to be overcome within Rover. To try to make his point, Martin-Hurst arranged for the competitions department to fit the engine he'd acquired from Mercury into a factory runabout P6. As an illustration of what he was up against, the people who should have done the job, the engineering department, complained they were too busy to mess about with it. Then, on the way back to the Midlands from a board meeting in London, in that particular V8-powered P6, Martin-Hurst invited Spencer Wilks to try it out. Wilks was astonished at what the engine did to the car, and Martin-Hurst received permission to go on his buying trip.

By January 1965 the initial confusion had been sorted (GM hadn't at first believed that Rover was serious) and agreement was reached. Rover could manufacture the V8 engine under licence. But, eager to get going, Rover had acquired all drawings and service records for the

engine before final agreement had been reached, and GM, anticipating the agreement, shipped 39 engines to Rover, taking Solihull's total to 40.

The 'Roverisation' programme

The engine required considerable development work before it was considered suitable for Rover applications, and the Rover people also had a lot to learn about a 90° V8, which was completely alien to their experience. To help them out the chief engine designer of GM's Buick division, Joe Turlay – who had headed the V8's original design team, and was therefore regarded as the engine's designer – moved over to Solihull. First application of the engine, now with a displacement of 3,528cc, was in the P5 in February 1966, the 3-litre straight six engine of which had never been entirely satisfactory. The V8 improved the rather stately P5 markedly, and, in turn, was destined to turn the P6 into one of Britain's greatest saloons when the Three Thousand Five was introduced as an additional model to the existing P6 'fours' in the spring of 1968. Meanwhile, over at Land Rover, the first of three 88-inch vehicles had been fitted with early examples of the V8 before the dark days of autumn 1966 had begun to bite. The Range Rover was more than three years away at this point, but its future engine was already starting to prove itself.

The full story of the development of the Range Rover, and the part the Buick-Rover V8 played, is told elsewhere in this book. However, it is worth noting here that the engine was operating perfectly satisfactorily in pre-production models before 1969; yet it was to be ten years before the Stage 1 Land Rovers appeared with essentially the same engine. All sorts of reasons have been given for this delay, such as cash constraints, the conservative nature of the market into which the Land

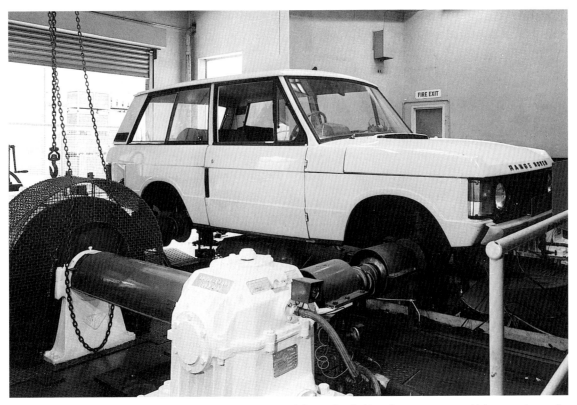

An important part of V8 engine testing was this unusual four-wheel drive dynamometer, which reproduces the effects of a moving car. (Rover Group/BMIHT/National Motor Museum)

The first utility model to be factory fitted with the 3.5-litre V8 engine was the Series III Stage 1, the first step towards the all-new coil-sprung model which was introduced in 1983. (National Motor Museum)

Rover was sold, and the inability of the people at Land Rover (it was always a small operation, remember) to get to grips with all the projects presented to them.

It is worth bearing in mind, too, that to some degree the Range Rover was doing the job for them. It was felt in some circles at Rover that if people wanted power and ride comfort the Range Rover was the vehicle for them; surely nobody wanted a working vehicle which didn't break your back every time you hit a bump and could do 80mph on any half-decent road? Yet in the Range Rover, Land Rover had developed what would prove to be the best 4×4 for 26 years without, in the beginning, really knowing who was likely to buy it. They had felt it would appeal to people who required an off-road working vehicle and then, after hosing out the interior, pop out in it for an evening at the opera. In their wildest dreams they didn't know they would create a new market with the Range Rover, as very rapidly proved the case. So any views anybody at Rover had about not giving power and comfort to the working Land Rover should have been treated with a pinch of salt by those who felt differently.

First V8 Land Rover

The V8-powered Stage 1, as already stated, was a result of investment and a decision to take the brakes off the company, and as such was a half-way house along the road to the development of an all-new Land Rover. The belated decision was made to put the Range Rover engine, transmission, suspension, and running gear beneath a Series III 109-inch body, a major step forward which ought to have happened at least five or six years earlier.

Not all V8-powered Series IIIs were working vehicles. This is the Stage 1 Carawagon Series 90, a high-powered, if thirsty, mobile home. (National Motor Museum)

This Range Rover was specially adapted by the factory to act as a mobile data gatherer to assist with the development of other cars. Here it is wired up to an early SD1 for test track work carried out at up to 100mph, something which would not have been possible without the V8 engine. (National Motor Museum)

The engine had required 'Roverisation' after its acquisition from General Motors, and had then required further modification for use in the Range Rover. For example, it had to be capable of running for 40 minutes without overheating with the vehicle at a standstill at a 45° angle, and it was felt essential that any engine used in an off-road machine wasn't complete unless it had a starting handle facility.

Principally because of the Land Rover's huge export market which, by definition, meant it had to be capable of operation in poorly developed countries where petrol quality was sometimes quite dreadful, the V8 had to be in a lower state of tune in the 109 than in the Range Rover from which it came. Yet it still gave 91bhp at a leisurely 3,500rpm, while the all-important torque figure was 166lb/ft at 2,000rpm, which was considerably more than the previous 'high-power' six-cylinder option, and quite out of the world when compared with the four-cylinder motors.

Fitting the V8 into the Series III, and changing over the transmission was not without its difficulties, as anyone who has

done their own conversion will readily testify, and it led to revision of the front-end panels to provide adequate all-round clearance for the engine. The set-back central grille section, one of the major visual characteristics of the Series III (and all that had gone before), was removed in favour of a flush front. Indeed, the front appearance of the Land Rover was, with these changes, quite similar to the frontal look which would eventually characterise the One Ten and Ninety, and then the Defender range.

Despite its somewhat stop-gap nature, the Stage 1 was a relatively successful vehicle, and began to make up some of the deficit, particularly in export markets, caused by the greater appeal (because of their power) of some of the opposition machinery. But this was nothing when compared with the effect the V8-powered One Ten, followed in turn by the Ninety, had on the world market.

From the launch of the One Ten, the V8 effectively received a new lease of life, and remained a popular choice through to the Defender 90 and 110 vehicles, before the Tdi became the only engine option,

The 3.5-litre V8 was an engine option in the Defender range for many years, giving levels of mechanical refinement with which the diesels can't compete.

other than on North American vehicles. But it remained, of course, the principal choice for the Range Rover, being developed firstly to 3.9 litres via a longer stroke – more in the interests of US users than the home market. This enlarged version was used in the Range Rover, with a 4.2-litre option available in the 108-inch LSE model for those who wanted even more from their V8. The 3.9 was also used in the Discovery, although initially the new vehicle had been powered by a carburettor-fed 3.5, then an injected 3.5, before the jump to 3.9 litres.

As already mentioned, major redevelopment work on the engine was a major part of the project which became the new Range Rover in 1994. It was completely redesigned and given a new block and management system, and a choice of 3,948cc for the 4.0 models and 4,554cc for the 4.6. Interestingly, the capacity of the 3.9 (as used in the Discovery) and 4.0-litre models is exactly the same.

Old the engine might be, but there's been nothing better since it was first put into the P5 saloon, despite the lack of interest shown by people at Rover when the very first one arrived at Solihull. Thank goodness for the foresight of William Martin-Hurst!

Chapter Nine

The Dunsfold treasure

The world's biggest treasure house of historically important Land Rovers is privately owned by the low-budget Dunsfold Land Rover Collection in Surrey. The vehicles represent the entire history of the Land Rover, yet have been assembled over the years mainly through the efforts of the Bashall family, who are among the greatest supporters the marque has ever had, or is likely to have.

The origins of the Collection date back to the late-1960s, when Brian Bashall established a small Land Rover business. Brian, an enthusiast for various types of classic vehicles, decided one day, more or less on a whim, to buy a military wading

This amphibious Land Rover is the machine with which Brian Bashall started the Dunsfold Collection. It still thrills the crowds with its antics across water.

Land Rover. He bought it simply because it appealed to him, and because he had a particular interest in unusual vehicles and the military applications of the Land Rover; a measure of the strength of this 'whim' is that he invested a third of his capital in it. This vehicle went on to become the foundation of an ever-growing collection of historical and unusual Land Rovers, and it still plays an active role, sometimes showing its swimming abilities to astonished crowds at displays. And no matter how many times people see it in action it never ceases to amaze them with its genuinely amphibious capabilities. Other odd vehicles followed this initial acquisition, and then Land Rover began to realise that Brian was serious about preserving historically significant machinery. Over a period of time, instead of breaking up prototypes, as was the custom, the factory began releasing them to Brian Bashall, and the world's greatest collection

of Land Rovers started taking shape.

The Dunsfold Land Rover Collection is administered by Brian and Philip Bashall, and Richard Beddall, at Alford Road, Dunsfold, Surrey, and depends on voluntary donations and volunteer assistance to keep it going. For a payment of £20 enthusiasts can become Friends of the Dunsfold Collection (details on 01483 200567). All the vehicles in the Collection are brought out for the annual open day, held in the first week of October. This event is open to everyone, and makes a wonderful day out for all Land Rover enthusiasts.

The vehicles are housed in a selection of barns, in the Dunsfold area and in other locations. It had been hoped that the Collection would acquire charity status which would, in turn, have attracted the necessary investment to turn it into more of a museum, but this dream has yet to be realised. To enter any of the barns is to

This fine line-up is just part of the Dunsfold Collection, photographed the morning after the annual Open Day at the Surrey site. In the foreground is a cutaway display Discovery, while facing the camera is Brian Bashall's superbly restored Series I.

walk into a treasure house containing some of the most historically significant vehicles produced by the Solihull company. It includes some which have played their part in saving Rover from possible financial disaster more than once, leading players in the success story which eventually led to BMW buying Rover. The Collection houses vehicles representing the beginnings of Land Rover, its recent past, and everything which has happened in between. Bringing it right up to date are two prototype Freelanders, diesel and petrol versions, along with the 'mule' which was used for engine, transmission, and suspension testing, clocking up a huge mileage in the process.

In a way, every vehicle on the Collection's books has its own unique story to tell, but it makes an interesting exercise to pull out some of the more significant ones representing the various facets of the Land Rover story over the years.

New Range Rover

Evidence of Dunsfold's present-day special relationship with Land Rover is abundantly clear in the now familiar shape of

The Dunsfold Collection includes an early, pre-production example of the new Range Rover. Here the author enjoys a spot of off-roading in it.

the new Range Rover which forms part of the Collection. This is a 38A, as the vehicle was designated by the factory, a pre-production car, completely unbadged, with an early chassis number. Apart from its prototype left-hand drive arrangement, it has a number of differences from production examples, including the air suspension set-up, which in its production form is one of the Range Rover's principal selling points.

Evidence of its development role can be seen very clearly on the windscreen, which carries a number of markings put on in the process of carrying out demisting and visibility angle tests. In the back is the canvas disguise kit used when it was taken out of the factory, and it has a full production style body, other than the bumper arrangement. It is a very early vehicle, chassis number 35, and is believed to have been driven around on G registration plates. The engine casting shows '4.5', which is something the 4,554cc version of the V8 (one of the Range Rover's two petrol options) was never known as, even experimentally.

If ever there was a classic in the making, this is it.

Velar

The importance of the Range Rover, a market leader throughout its lifetime, cannot be overstated. Among the three pre-production examples – all badged Velar, of course – normally to be found at Dunsfold is trustee Richard Beddall's very original one. It is in lovely condition, both bodily and mechanically, and had a gearbox overhaul in 1997; interestingly, it is one of the few Velars still in everyday use. Most are used regularly, but not many work in the way this one does. It has received a fair bit of upgrading over the years, but still retains all its original mechanical components. This

Velar is YVB 171, and the other two in the Trust's care are YVB 162 and YVB 172. It is one of a batch of management assessment vehicles which performed a key role in the development of the project before production began for the 1970 launch. Another interesting Range Rover held is the prototype ambulance; it was actually the last of the Range Rover prototypes, converted specially to an ambulance body.

The first road test of the Range Rover was published in *Autocar*, and featured a beige vehicle which is also now owned by the Collection. This Range Rover is the first to be badged as such, and has chassis number 49.

Range Rover engine test bed

One of Dunsfold's Land Rovers played an important part in the development of the V8 engine which was crucial to the success of the Range Rover, and which is still used, in a highly revised form, in the very latest Range Rovers. The vehicle is a red Series IIA which was used as the principal mobile test bed for the 3.5-litre engine Rover had eventually acquired from Buick after the trip by William Martin-Hurst to the USA in early-1964. Three Series IIA 88-inch models were taken off the production line and fitted with early versions of the V8. They then went out to cover very high mileages to assess the engine in advance of its first production installation in the P5, before taking on other work.

One of the key engineers involved in the project was Geof Miller, who was later to be the project engineer for the original Range Rover in the late-1960s. This particular Land Rover was the one used by Geof in the course of his engine testing, and was somewhat upgraded for the purpose. The thoroughness of the testing carried out in this machine, along

This is the 88-inch Land Rover used by Geof Miller and his team as a mobile test bed for the V8 engine as part of the Roverisation and development programme. There is a photograph of the engine bay on page 114.

with the other two, helped to ensure that the V8 went into production firstly in the P5 in 1966, then the following year in the P6, and finally in the Range Rover. Without it the Range Rover might not have been the fantastic success it turned out to be, saving the Rover company's bacon on more than one occasion.

This IIA can still be driven today despite its rather poor condition. Impressive, instantly, is the state of the prototype V8 in its engine bay. It has a bite to equal its impressive bark, and despite its age and the various duties it has been called upon to perform, has the unrivalled combination of power, torque, and smoothness which has ensured the ex-Buick engine's place in British motoring history.

First Series II Station Wagon

Found among the motoring ads in a free newspaper published in Wiltshire was the earliest Series II Station Wagon, built in 1958, carrying chassis number 1. It still has the original works registration number, and possesses countless distinctive features. It is completely original, a ten-seater as opposed to having 12 seats, and has been upgraded over the years by having a later heater and servo assisted brakes fitted, although it still features the early vent control knobs and wipers, and has its original engine, gearbox, axles, and even radiator. Although it joined the Dunsfold fleet carrying a current MoT and road tax, it is in urgent need of restoration, which, because of its historical

This is the very first Series II Station Wagon, carrying chassis number 1. It was acquired by the Dunsfold Collection in 1997 after being advertised in a local newspaper, and came complete with MoT and full service history. It is now awaiting full restoration.

importance, will have to be correct in all original details.

First Series III

All production Land Rovers have been successful, but perhaps the most familiar leaf-sprung model is the Series III, launched in 1971 and still a familiar sight on our roads. The very first Series III lives in the Dunsfold barns and a recent opportunity to take it off-roading, and drive it around the country lanes of Surrey, was a great privilege. Proudly wearing chassis number 1, this 1970 Land Rover hides its glories beneath a coat of sombre grey paint. Like virtually all prototypes, it was originally left-hand drive, but was con-

verted to a right hooker at an early stage in order to permit fitment of the Rover 2200 overhead cam engine, more commonly found in the P6 saloon. The engine wouldn't fit around the left-drive steering box, so conversion to right-hand drive was essential if the engine was to be assessed in the Land Rover.

It is delightfully original. Even the radiator hoses are dated 1971, and it was converted back to its proper Station Wagon configuration after being purchased from the John Craddock collection some time ago. It has not been restored, yet is in surprisingly good condition and even has a current MoT. Driving it for a special feature in *Land Rover Owner* magazine was a special treat – particularly so because it enabled me to find out for myself why Rover very wisely decided not to go ahead with fitting the P6 engine in production Series III models. Its power characteristics would have made it just about the world's worst off-roader and a pretty abysmal tow vehicle, although once it gets up to speed it cruises delightfully on main roads.

Second Ninety prototype

The most familiar machines to most people among the fabulous Dunsfold Collection are the Trust's three prototype Ninetys. Furthermore, not content simply to have three prototypes of the world's most respected and best known 4×4, the Collection has the first three to be manufactured. The historical importance of this trio of Land Rovers cannot be measured.

The second of these prototypes is in lovely condition, despite being used year-round, sometimes as a hack vehicle. I have driven it myself, including a pretty serious off-roading session, in which it performed so well it could almost have been a very much younger Defender. Like other prototype Ninetys it began life as a very early One Ten. Launched in early-1983, the One Ten was the first Land Rover (as opposed to Range Rover) to have coil springs, and was in production for a year before the Ninety, as it was then named, was introduced after having been developed from it.

Significantly, the second prototype was the first to be built with the wheelbase actually used in production, 92.9 inches. Prototype No 1 was built with a wheelbase of precisely 90in, but this was found to give insufficient body length. This significant second prototype has a cut-down One Ten roof, with extended hard-top from a Series III 88-inch model. The fuel filler is raised up in the Series III position, it has a 109 V8 radiator grille, Range

Rover axles, and Range Rover style permanent four-wheel drive (as opposed to No 1's optional 4×4 system). Originally, it had a 2.25-litre petrol engine, as fitted to Series IIIs, but Dunsfold have installed a normally aspirated 2.5-litre diesel, making it a much better off-roader. They

The second Ninety prototype in the Collection still has the fuel filler in the Series III position, and the joins where the body was extended from an 88 can be clearly seen.

still have the original engine, though, in case they ever want to return it to its former state.

110 Bonneted Control

One of the more unusual vehicles in the Collection is the 1966 110 Bonneted Control, or the Big Lightweight as some incorrectly call it, which was designed as an artillery tractor in a private venture by Rover. It was built to tow a power-driven trailer and a gun; the trailer would have been the limber, with the gun behind it. It's a bit wider than a normal 110, although it still has the narrow ENV axles, making it look very 'narrow gutted', and it is extremely low-geared.

In a way, it's a sort of 101 Forward Control, but with a bonnet. It has a Rover 3-litre car engine, as in the P5. The artillery tractor plan fell flat on its face, and the machine was being used to tow gang mowers around the factory site before Dunsfold acquired it, and thereby saved it from obscurity. Perhaps the only good thing about it is that it was one of the first Land Rovers to have a five-speed gearbox. It has a twin transfer box arrangement to give it low drive and high in power-driven trailer mode. Unfortunately, it has lousy steering, lousy gearing, and lousy brakes ... and there is no other way to describe them. Not all Land Rover enthusiasts agree that Dunsfold did the right thing in saving it!

127/129

Known to everyone at Dunsfold as Lofty, the Collection includes what is known more formally as a 127 or 129, one of five such vehicles specially built in 1962 as a potential export machine for various African states. It was trialled against the Unimog in Belgium, and unfortunately the Unimog walked all over it. It has a 35cwt

capacity, and this preserved model was the only one to be fitted with a CAV turbocharged and intercooled version of the 2.5-litre Land Rover diesel engine. It has a five-bearing block, unheard of in the early-1960s when it was built, but without those five bearings the engine simply would not have taken the power. Interestingly, the engine was later used as the basis for the development of the production five-bearing units of the late-1970s.

Only one other Lofty survives, with rounded wings and a 3-litre car engine. It languishes in the Heritage Museum at Gaydon.

Belgian 2×4

Among the more pointless Land Rovers ever made are some two-wheel drive 88-inch vehicles, of which there is one in the Dunsfold Collection. It was from a batch of between 150 and 250 88s built for the Belgian Government in 1974 as part of a car contract, the idea being to have non-specialist vehicles which could utilise the parts for the Land Rovers the Belgians had in service when maintenance was required. These rather futile Land Rovers were used mainly by the Belgian police for general road work. They were radio equipped, and therefore 24 volts, and even had special miniature blackout lights.

Batches of them have been released by the Belgian authorities and began to appear in Britain from early 1997. In fact they have more than purely curiosity value, since they provide everything people like about conventional Land Rovers other than four-wheel drive, which is not a problem for urban-based enthusiasts.

100-inch automatic

An exceptionally unusual vehicle, and one which is fascinating to drive because of its transmission arrangement, is the 1978

It might look as though it is run by a firm of builders, but this is the Collection's Trans Americas Expedition Range Rover, complete with bridge-making ladders.

prototype of a batch of 100-inch models made specially for the Swiss Army. Not only is it the only 100-inch Land Rover-styled body ever made, but it also has a three-speed automatic gearbox with a chain-driven transfer box, specially requested by the Swiss, the only Land Rover ever made with an auto box. The doors and modified panels were produced by Jensen.

Unfortunately, the combination of standard 2.25-litre petrol engine, large, heavy body, and three-speed automatic transmission ensure it wouldn't win any races. It is difficult to imagine it climbing Swiss mountains during pre-production trials, too. In the event it didn't matter. The Swiss never actually bought any of them, in retaliation for Margaret Thatcher's gov-

ernment refusing to sanction the purchase of some Swiss training aircraft. Only 15 of these 100-inch vehicles were produced, and Dunsfold also has a soft-top version. Other models still surviving include a soft-top station wagon. This particular one has four comfortable seats with rifle stowage, and two jump seats in the rear.

1951 80-inch

Despite the great historical importance of most of the exhibits, for many enthusiasts the star of the Dunsfold Collection is Brian Bashall's 1951 Series I 80-inch, which has been fully restored by Geoffrey Cousins, for a long time one of Britain's leading custom car builders. He found the vehicle in a dreadful state and decided to return it to factory condition. After discussions he was given a free run of the stores of the commercial Land Rover business at Dunsfold, taking whatever he needed to rebuild it. At one time it was going to be sold to an American collector, but Dunsfold trustee Brian Bashall pointed out it was too nice to sell, and then bought it!

It is totally correct in every detail and a truly authentic restoration of a Series I of the time, apart from the shiny paint, especially beneath the bonnet, where to truly replicate the original it would simply be 'dusted' over. Anyone wishing to see a very early Land Rover as it would have been as a new vehicle could do far worse than inspect this particular vehicle.

NAS 88-inch

A 1970 US specification 88-inch, probably the last one to be registered by Land Rover as a demonstrator, makes an interesting comparison with the European machinery. It is finished in the usual American red. Power comes from a normal 2.25-litre petrol engine, although notable differences from a British 88-inch model include power sapping emission pack, 15-inch (instead of 16-inch) wheels, larger flasher lamps, side marker lamps, full de-luxe trim, and different heater. The vehicle has always lived in Britain and had been owned by an enthusiast, who passed it on to the Collection.

Land Rover sales in the USA ceased in 1974 because of inability to comply with safety and emissions legislation. This is a Federal 88 Station Wagon, built for the American market in 1970, but never shipped there. Interestingly, at that time you could only buy a red Land Rover in the USA.

You don't see many vehicles like this six-wheeled, left-hand drive Range Rover around town!

Llama

Dunsfold's rarities are not confined to the more generally recognisable Land Rover vehicles. For instance, there are two Llama trucks, a development vehicle with which it had been hoped to replace the military 101 in the mid-1980s. Eleven prototypes were built, but unfortunately the vehicle was never accepted by the Army. It has the 3.5-litre Rover V8 engine, a five-speed Santana gearbox, coil spring suspension, glass fibre tilting cab, and is a real joy to drive. There is actually a production version of the Llama at the Heritage Motor Museum at Gaydon, Warwickshire, which is much more refined than Dunsfold's pre-production examples.

101 Forward Control

The Collection owns the left-hand drive 101 Forward Control wearing LHD chassis number 1 as well as right-hand drive number 1, and there are various other low-number 101s in different forms, several with very low chassis numbers. The 101 has been a key vehicle with the armed forces. Power comes from a V8 Range Rover engine, fitted with the shortened bellhousing Range Rover gearbox, and they have 900x16 wheels and Land Rover long wheelbase brakes. They're delightful to drive, and make brilliant off-roaders. Among Dunsfold's collection of 101s are the prototype ambulance and Challenger crane (a REME fitters' vehicle) plus numerous others.

Chapter Ten

Land Rovers on parade

Although Maurice and Spencer Wilks never envisaged their Land Rover project as a military vehicle, at least not in the early stages, it was inevitable that a lightweight British four-wheel drive utility vehicle would appeal to the armed forces. This was especially so since the Land Rover was being developed less than two years after the end of the Second World War, in which the Willys and Ford Jeeps had played such an important part. Coincidence, which pops up in the best-regulated circles, also came into the picture. As early as 1943 the British Army had come up with a plan, albeit embryonic, which involved the development of a home-built lightweight 4×4. It was, as is often the case with military schemes, a complicated plan which involved a number of manufacturers co-operating in what was envisaged as a protracted programme of initial development.

So when the authorities got to hear what was going on at Rover, and with their own machine still way over the horizon, they arranged for three pre-production Land Rovers to be made available for evaluation. It looked like an answer to all their problems and, fortunately for Rover's fortunes for decades to come, this proved to be the case. An order went in requesting delivery of a batch of 50 for the year after the launch, with a repeat order for even more. But there was a hiccup at the beginning which, had it turned out otherwise, might have put a totally different complexion on Land Rover's relationship with the military. The Army's own project, coded FV1800, was to be powered by the Rolls-Royce four-cylinder B40 engine, and in the interests of conformity the Army thought that any Land Rovers they had might be a better bet if they had the B40 under the bonnet, rather than the 1,595cc Rover unit.

Consequently a batch of 30 or so Land Rovers were built with the Rolls-Royce engine, not by Land Rover but by Hudson Motors of London. Unfortunately, it was not an easy marriage, and led to the generally little-known but, paradoxically, much talked-about '81-inch' models. Extensive modification was required to accommodate the Rolls-Royce engine, including repositioning the rear springs and shock absorbers (hence 81-inch), and the end result was never fully satisfactory. It was too much of a compromise. The radiator filler cap even came up through the bonnet. Then came crucial field trials, to which Land Rover sent a standard production vehicle to be set against the 81-inch and an early FV1800 (with Rolls-Royce engine, of course), which had progressed to the prototype stage and would later go into production as the Austin Champ.

Land Rover enthusiasts with an interest in history know the rest. The standard Land Rover out-performed everything else, including the B40-engined 81-inch, despite the fact that the complete vehicle had cost less than just one of the Rolls-Royce engines! It was a significant beginning to Land Rover's career as a military vehicle manufacturer, and further proof – not that it was needed – that the design of the original vehicle was nothing short of brilliant inspiration.

Further confirmation of this can be found in the fact that a great many of the Land Rovers which have served Queen and country, and which have rallied to the flags of dozens of other nations, have been standard or near-standard vehicles. Over the years they've been fitted for radio (VFR), been adapted as gun carriers, ambulances, workshops, fire engines, mobile starters for helicopters and fixed wing aircraft, command vehicles, load carriers, personnel carriers, light support vehicles, and general runabouts, but beneath the skin they have remained close to their civilian counterparts.

Enter the Lightweight

A great step forward in military Land Rovers came when the so-called

It is no longer in military hands, but this Lightweight is very much at home as it makes a river crossing. The Lightweight is one of the most enthusiastically supported of all Land Rovers. (National Motor Museum)

Lightweight, or air portable, entered service in 1968, although the first had been built for evaluation some three years earlier. And we have an unusual version of a quirky little French car, the Citroën 2CV, to thank for events which led to the development by Land Rover of one of its best-loved vehicles.

A pick-up version of the Citroën had been tried as a helicopter-delivered support vehicle for the Marine Commandos in the late-1950s but, not surprisingly, it was not robust enough. Unfortunately all current Land Rovers, even when stripped out, were too heavy to be lifted by the helicopters of the period, but eventually the 88-inch Lightweight came along and saved the day. Its unique appearance, with squared-off wheelarches and plain body panels, has developed a passionate following among modern enthusiasts, after many

years of great service in the ranks. It is a delightful machine with a great deal more character than most Land Rovers. In nominating it as my own favourite from all the utility vehicles the company has ever built I am far from being alone.

Another highly popular military machine with non-military Land Rover people today is the Forward Control, which came into being because the Army wanted a machine to carry the sort of loads a normal long wheelbase Land Rover just wasn't capable of. Trials in the late-1960s with military versions of the civilian 109-inch Forward Control, and then a 110-inch model, were unsuccessful because the standard 2.25 engines were hopelessly out of the reckoning in terms of power. But Rover knew something that their critics didn't – the Rover V8 engine, by then being used in Rover saloons and already

The Military 101 Forward Control provided exceptional ability over bad terrain, and it could also be used in conjunction with the powered-axle trailer, as seen here. (National Motor Museum)

Forward Control 101s make an imposing sight whenever they are lined up, military style, at shows and displays.

being finally sorted for use in the impending Range Rover, was likely to prove ideal for the 4×4 load carrier and gun tug required by the Army.

The wizards at Land Rover knew that the Range Rover engine and transmission would work in this new application, and it was not at all difficult for them to design the right bodywork to go around it, taking the military's requirements for tough off-roading, load carrying, and road work into account. It was a true Forward Control, thereby utilising the vehicle's overall dimensions to the full, and totally spartan in the best traditions of the military. It had massive ground clearance and, although it used semi-elliptic springs rather than the coils supporting the Range Rover, it was a stunning off-road machine.

It was, of course, the much-admired and much-loved 101, exhibited to the world for the first time at the 1972 Commercial Motor Show, and remained a hard-worked military machine for many years despite only being manufactured until 1978. Its life was cut short because civilian orders were not forthcoming, perhaps not surprisingly given its incredibly basic nature and, in everyday terms, impractical character.

It has been estimated that as many as 40–43 per cent of all leaf-sprung Land Rovers ever built were bought by military and quasi-military establishments around the world, even finding their way into the barracks of some countries possessing, to say the least, strained relations with Britain.

Coils for the forces

Of course, Land Rover's relationships with the armed forces of much of the world didn't stop with the change from leaf springing to coils in 1983 and 1984; if anything, the opposite occurred, and as the 110 and 90 were developed their better off-road ability and superior on-road performance endeared them even more to people in uniform.

The military is inclined to hang on to its vehicles much longer than civilian operators. It is necessary for them to have very large stocks of spares to provide independence in emergency situations and, of course, to be able to carry on in the event of a cessation of production at the factory for any reason. Furthermore, it is essential to keep large numbers of reserve vehicles 'just in case', and this means that leaf-sprung vehicles continued in service for a great many years after the launch of the coil sprung machines and, indeed, some leaf-sprung Series III vehicles are still in service in Britain and around the world.

But the Defender is a great favourite with countless armies, navies and air forces because of its even greater versatility, and all manner of adaptations have been carried out to both chassis types to fit them for active duty. The 'stretched' 110, initially labelled as the 127 before acquiring its current 130 label, and most familiar to civilians as the High-Capacity Pick-up and Crew Cab vehicle, has proved to be a particularly useful machine. One of its most universal roles has been as an ambulance, serving for the first time in the Gulf War, although not in great numbers since it was only just coming into service at the time. Since then it has starred (if that's the right expression) in much of the television coverage of the war in the former Yugoslavia, wearing United Nations white paintwork. It's an excellent support vehicle, being fully air-portable, enormously versatile, and sharing the parts bins of all the other Defenders.

In its Crew Cab version the 130 makes an ideal vehicle for pulling field guns, a job it does exceptionally well, and considerably more efficiently than the Series III 109-inch which did the job for many years without too many complaints. Other jobs include working as a missile tractor, general load and personnel carrying, and providing humanitarian services in hot-spots such as Bosnia. One of the main medical uses has been as an airfield crash ambulance, a role in which it has proved far more effective than the earlier 109-inch four-stretcher ambulance, and considerably more useful than the single-stretcher Range Rover ambulance.

It was no coincidence that the V8 engine which provided the power for the Range Rover fast response fire tender was also used in the airfield ambulance variant of the 130, enabling it to get to crash sites rapidly – airfields can be very large places – and then operate at very high road speeds during the evacuation of casualties.

Pinkies and Dinkies

Most glamorous of the military applications of Land Rovers has always been when working in earnest for the SAS and Long Range Desert Group, and you'll always find crowds clustered around any vehicles appearing at shows in the colours and equipment of these units. There's been a continuous relationship between Land Rover and these elite units since the 1950s, when they first adapted Series Is for their unique operations and found they liked them very much. Perhaps the best known of their vehicles are the highly equipped 109-inch 'Pink Panthers' (or Pinkies), thus known from their desert camouflage. Bristling with guns, but otherwise well stripped, these just have to be the most menacing of all the Solihull vehicles which have seen active service.

Good though the Series IIs were (there were never any Series III Pinkies), they

The guns might be deactivated and the cartridges dummies, but long-range patrol vehicles always create a daunting impression. Youngsters of all ages love them!

were not a patch on the Desert Patrol Vehicles which were developed from High Capacity 110s. Mostly these were V8 powered, although there were some with diesel engines, and a number of 90s were also fitted out on a variation of the same theme.

The Gulf War (1990–91) provided Land Rover with a huge public relations boost with the military. Thousands of Land Rovers in just about every configuration were shipped out, and they performed superbly. Everybody involved was impressed (probably Saddam Hussein's forces more than anybody!) and among

those smitten were the American Special Forces, the US Rangers. They had seen how the SAS was able to perform with its stripped-out 110 gunship Pink Panthers, and they wanted them. In fact such were the demands put on the vehicles by the SAS themselves that they used up all their available 110s, leading to the rapid conversion of some 90s to fill the breach. Perhaps inevitably, with the 110s being known as Pinkies, the short wheelbase machines were instantly dubbed 'Dinkies'.

In the year following the Gulf War Land Rover announced a new Special Operations Vehicle, derived directly from

This half-track arrangement instead of four wheels provided exceptional mobility in the most adverse conditions. It was seen in military terms as, primarily, a bomb disposal machine. (National Motor Museum)

those used in the desert, and the US Rangers were among the first customers, with a batch of V8-powered vehicles. Land Rover also produced them with diesel engines.

Multi Role Combat Vehicles

But for all the glamour of the SAS machinery, the widest use of Defenders in the British Forces has been as a Multi Role Combat Vehicle, the Land Rovers proving ideal for the various roles demanded for the many situations with which the Services find themselves having to deal. The three types of Defender are all used in this many-faceted application, in which the various body types, depending on the actual job to be done, are added to a basic rolling chassis. It couldn't be simpler and the low cost of doing it appeals greatly to cost-conscious units and the specialist conversion companies employed. In many ways it brings the military Land Rover right back to the original principle of the vehicle when it was being designed in 1947: a supremely versatile working machine capable of doing any job asked of it.

Forget the more glamorous applications

for a while, because this is what the military Land Rovers have always been best at. True, nothing could overshadow the reliability and go-anywhere versatility of the SAS 109s and 110s, but thousands of Land Rovers work every day for the British Army (and a great many other armies) carrying out very routine tasks which no other vehicle in the world would be as suitable for, despite the often mundane nature of the work.

The story, of course, continues, with various specialist Land Rovers being developed following the introduction of the MRCV. Most significant is the Wolf, or XD Defender (for e**X**tra **D**uty), which was given the go-ahead in 1996 following a prolonged trials and development programme aimed at finding an extra-tough vehicle in both 110 and 90 formats. It is an incredibly strong and durable vehicle, intended for arduous front-line duties, and is expected to be in service for as long as 12–15 years. Developed in parallel was the Pulse ambulance project, built around the 130 base vehicle and, like the Wolf, using the 300 Tdi engine. This, too, was given the green light in early-1996, and the total order for both Wolf and Pulse amounted to 8,800 vehicles. Given the fact that it has been conclusively proved there is no better vehicle anywhere in the world for military purposes, the 50-year relationship between the British Army, plus others around the world (some of them for almost as long), is as sure to continue as night follows day.

However, as Land Rover discovered when developing the latest military machines, the requirements of the services are becoming tougher with every fresh tender for new vehicles. It takes a special kind of company to be able to satisfy the demands of the military, and it is only

The Defender XD 130 is the most effective military ambulance to see service with the British forces. (National Motor Museum)

All the intimate secrets of the Defender XD 110 24-volt hard-top are revealed here, including the tough internal cage. (National Motor Museum)

because the base vehicles are so good that the outlook is bright for Land Rover in this crucial part of its business.

The Boys in Blue

Land Rover's relationship with Britain's police forces is, in some ways, as important as the company's defence business. Police orders don't bring in anything like the cash generated by military vehicles, but Land Rovers, Discoverys, and Range Rovers used by the police have the highest imaginable profile. And this means a higher level of civilian business than would be the case if there were no police cars wearing the Land Rover badge. The public recognise that police forces would not order vehicles if they were not up to the job.

Land Rovers have served with the police since the early days, when some rural forces bought them for cross country work and, in the case of areas particularly prone to bad winter conditions, to give

the best possible chance of year-round mobility. Initially, with the exception of parts of Scotland, Wales and some of the hillier districts of England, some forces perhaps had only one Land Rover, and some had none at all. But over the years the idea caught on, and even urban forces now usually have at least a Defender or two to call on. Throughout Scotland, Wales, Cumbria, Northumberland, Yorkshire, and the Peak District police Land Rovers are extremely numerous, while even in flatter parts of the country it is not at all unusual for rural beat officers to be issued with a Defender.

Traffic departments loved the Range Rover when they first evaluated the vehicle after its launch in 1970. It was almost everything the traffic officer could wish for, with 100mph (161kmh) capability, room for five people, plenty of load space, and the ability to keep going in deep snow and across fields. They learned to live with the body roll, more pronounced with all the police equipment

It is far from a military vehicle, but this Discovery is one of many around the world which have been converted into paramedic urgent response vehicles. (National Motor Museum)

aboard than in most civilian applications, and it would be years before the police had to worry about fuel costs. The Range Rover became one of Britain's principal traffic department vehicles, alongside, for many years, another excellent Rover product, the SD1 saloon. The police loved the original version, and grew to like it even more as it progressed over the years, and there were many long faces when it was learned that the Classic was to be phased out. Those lucky enough to have the new Range Rover, though, are not at all unhappy, because it is even more suited for police work than the original. The more powerful engines, extra space, and improved handling are much appreciated.

Some forces have used Discoverys as highway patrol vehicles with great success, provided they've been V8-powered. Unfortunately, loaded down with communications equipment and all the gear car-ried these days, particularly on motorway work, the Tdi versions are less satisfactory. As one officer with experience of using a Tdi Discovery on motorways told me, 'It is embarrassing to be driving flat out to an incident, blue lights and siren switched on, to find ordinary cars passing you every time you come to a hill!' But for more everyday situations the Discovery has fared well in police hands. I spent a day with the Cambridgeshire force, riding in one of their Discoverys, and was impressed with the way it coped with general road work and a considerable amount of off-roading.

Land Rovers are also popular with HM Coastguard, providing access to cliff tops and mobility on headlands and beaches, and they are also used enthusiastically by the Customs and Excise. Other users include the Ambulance Service and Mountain Rescue organisations, for whom there are very obvious benefits.

Chapter Eleven

Choosing and buying a Land Rover

Those of us who have been around Land Rovers for some time know what we want when it comes to choosing a new one. But the situation is very different for the ever-growing number of people finding themselves attracted to the world's best 4×4 for the first time, or anyone branching out from one type of Land Rover to a model of which they have no previous experience.

Which vehicle to go for is a complex question in which a number of factors play their part. These include:

— The amount of cash available.
— What the vehicle will be used for.
— The anticipated annual mileage.
— Whether you are looking for a new or a used vehicle.
— Whether you are looking for a modern or classic vehicle.
— Your own mechanical ability.

Some Land Rover machinery, such as Range Rovers from the mid- to late-'eighties, represents particularly good value for money, while late-model Defenders depreciate slowly and can therefore be expensive. Both cases illustrate vividly the need to proceed with great caution. A seemingly inexpensive Range Rover might as well be a hole in the ground waiting for you to throw your

money in if it has a rotten chassis, an engine which is past it, and badly worn transmission, suspension, brakes, and steering. I'm not joking or exaggerating, because this is a perfect description of a great many older Range Rovers. And that shiny Defender 90, which you feel sure will make excellent family transport, may prove totally unsuitable once the initial euphoria of owning it has worn off. Inward-facing rear seats are not a safe place for your children, there's nowhere to secure a baby seat, and when you're all in place there's no space for luggage.

So how do you sort through the huge choice of different vehicles available? Before getting hung up on any particular type of machine – unless, of course, you really do know precisely what you want – it's worth looking at what to expect from the different types of Land Rover in terms of condition and usability.

Classic Land Rovers

Land Rovers have been built since 1947 (if you include the prototypes), and it is

RIGHT Anyone looking for the perfect combination of comfort for the family, economy, long-distance cruising ability, and first-class off-roading could do a lot worse than a Discovery. Prices of used vehicles have become very reasonable, putting Discoverys within the reach of many enthusiasts.

widely accepted that all the leaf-sprung models falling into the Series I, Series II and Series III types are classics. Obviously, though, the further back you go the more classic they become.

Series I (1948–58)

This was the original and the best in the view of a great many enthusiasts, and who are we to argue? The first Land Rovers are best treated, these days, like most other venerable classics of their period, which means keeping them in top condition to ensure they live for ever, and restricting their use to weekends, rallies, shows and other special occasions. That said, the Series I Land Rover is capable of most things its later leaf-sprung brethren are, so it's a handy vehicle to have in case of heavy winter snowfalls. Mind you, the absence of a heater, or at best the presence of a very ineffective one, combined with the canvas sides and top common to many Series Is, means that winter motoring is only for the hardy.

All Series Is other than the diesels have overhead inlet and side exhaust (ioe) valve engines, and progress is slowest of all with the earliest version (1948–52), which had a 1.6-litre engine. The 2-litre engine from 1952 onwards was quite a lot better, but with both types you really can't expect to cruise at much more than 40–45mph (64–72kph), especially if you wish to respect the age of the engine and transmission. And they have poor brakes.

Purest of the Series Is, and for my money the best-looking Land Rover of the lot, is the 80-inch model, its very short wheelbase giving it a most appealing, toy-like appearance. The 80-inch was only made until 1954, and a great many have been used for trialling over the years, and trialling involves modification and abuse, reducing the stock of pure 80s. However, if you're a classic enthusiast and you fancy owning an original which will never lose value, and for which there will always be a buyer if you decide to sell, go for an 80-inch if you can find one at the right price. Other Series I wheelbases were 86-inch, 88-inch, 107-inch, and 109-inch, of which the 88-inch and 109-inch were capable of taking the 2,052cc diesel engine for which the wheelbase had to be extended by two inches.

Station Wagons have always been popular variants, and the first one was introduced on the 107-inch chassis (from 1955). The Station Wagon is really the only Series I Land Rover which is suitable for family use, and early versions are particularly revered. However, be careful if you're buying one of these to restore, especially if the body needs extensive renewal, because you could well find yourself involved in having to make up, or get made, quite a lot of the bodywork, unless you're very lucky.

Generally speaking the restoration of Series Is is steadily becoming more difficult as the supply situation for some of the parts dwindles. The restoration itself is not especially hard for anyone with reasonable mechanical knowledge and the ability to use welding equipment, and there are always enthusiasts willing to pass on the knowledge of their own experience.

Series I Land Rovers have long been a part of the general classic car scene, as well as the focal point of the Land Rover enthusiast movement, and it is most encouraging to know that new owners willing to restore and save them are coming along all the time. Perhaps you'll be one of them.

Series II and IIA (1958–71)

With the introduction of the Series II, Land Rover signalled a policy of evolution, rather than revolution, which was to last into the late-1990s. Wheelbases remained at 88-inch and 109-inch and the familiar shape was retained, although the so-called barrel sides, slightly curvier bonnet, 'modesty skirts' on the lower sides, and a 1.5-inch (38mm) increase in overall width made them look larger and more modern. By far the greatest improvement, however, was the introduction of the first overhead valve petrol engine, the 2,286cc unit which was destined to serve (with on-going improvements) into the 1980s. This engine was, in fact, not quite as new as some people believed – and still believe – because it was actually a development of the 2,052cc diesel unit already in use. Of course, it was modified for petrol use, and the cylinder head had received the attentions of tuning expert Harry Weslake. It was a large improvement over the previous 2-litre engine (which continued to be fitted to the 88-inch model until stocks were exhausted), and it is this petrol engine more than anything else which makes the Series II, IIA and III vehicles so much more usable than the Series I.

The two-and-a-quarter petrol engine, as it is known universally, is an extremely good unit. It is extraordinarily reliable and will soak up abuse which would destroy lesser engines; although it is not recommended, of course, this engine will forgive missed oil changes and harsh operating conditions more than any other engine ever made. This is important to today's enthusiast, because a seriously neglected and worn petrol engine will soldier on for a surprisingly long time; and then when the inevitable finally happens and it refuses to co-operate any more, the simple design ensures that even a full rebuild is not troublesome.

Series II and IIA Land Rovers are perhaps the ideal compromise between the older Series Is and more modern machin-

Don't fall into the mistake of thinking that Land Rovers don't rust. As this picture shows, they rust badly as they get older. This Series IIA needs a replacement chassis outrigger as well as a new floor and toe board section.

ery. They are undoubtedly classic, which gives them special appeal, and all of them can be used (at the time of writing) as road tax exempt. A petrol-engined series II or IIA in good condition, especially when fitted with the option Fairey overdrive, can be used for long road journeys, with a cruising speed of 55mph (88kph) or so and fuel consumption of about 21–23mpg.

Better manoeuvrability also came with the Series II, the extra body width permitting a wide track, which in turn enabled Land Rover to give the vehicles a better steering lock. Given the effort involved in shunting the steering around in tight situations this was most welcome, while anybody off-roading a long wheelbase model appreciates the tighter lock in awkward circumstances, even though it is still not as good as the much later 110. The Series II (and later) Land Rovers also ride a little better than Series Is, thanks to slightly lower spring rates and redesigned dampers. Repositioning the rear springs increased the rear suspension travel a bit, improving off-road performance.

The diesel engines were improved around the time the Series II was introduced, but it has to be said that the then current diesel unit was considerably inferior to the petrol engine and – most unusually – less reliable. Unless you're a diesel enthusiast, there is no great advantage in having a diesel-powered Series Land Rover, even with the much better 2,286cc unit introduced with the Series IIA (1962 model year). The later engine is a much more capable unit than the first type, but it is still a very noisy unit producing only 62bhp compared with the petrol unit's 77bhp. The only exception, really, is if you intend using your Land Rover for regular off-roading, in which case the diesel's flat torque curve, with its maximum of 103lb/ft at 1,800rpm, is much more suitable than the petrol

engine's 124lb/ft at 2,500rpm. And, of course, there is the benefit which you get with all diesels – there is no ignition system to fall prey to deep water and other wet conditions.

The popular truck cab was introduced with the Series II and this body style makes the 88-inch vehicle particularly good-looking. If you intend using a Land Rover one-up or two-up and have no need of a (relatively) secure load area, a truck cab 88-inch or 109-inch can be a most attractive proposition.

Another great body style, the Station Wagon, took a step forward in the autumn of 1958 when the 109-inch version became available. Land Rover had taken the opportunity of the longer wheelbase to smarten and tidy the Station Wagon, and it was now a much nicer vehicle than the Series I type. A Series II or IIA 109-inch Station Wagon is an extremely usable machine which proved very popular in its time, and still makes sense today, being arguably the very best of the classic Land Rover body variants. The 88-inch Station Wagon is also a fine-looking vehicle, although less practical when it comes to carrying people.

Series III (1971–85)

The Series III Land Rovers carried on where the IIAs had left off, with minor changes to the body and a distinctive new grille. But there were other changes which made the new model more pleasant to drive and a little more comfortable. The most welcome improvement was the introduction, at last, of an all-synchromesh gearbox, and this alone makes the Series III more suitable for those drivers today who have never had to cope without synchromesh. Up to this point there had only been synchromesh on third and fourth gears, something of a handicap when towing a caravan or horse-box, during which it is necessary to make frequent down changes into second and first gears.

Clutch life was extended with the standard fitment of the 9.5-inch unit hitherto only available on diesel and six-cylinder models. Much stronger half-shafts were fitted to the 109-inch version, following frequent breakages on Series IIs, and braking performance was also increased. Inside, there was a new facia with a full-width parcel shelf between padded crash rails, and the instruments were grouped directly in front of the driver. Instrumentation and controls were now almost to the same standard as those found in saloon cars of the time.

The popular Station Wagon concept was taken a stage further with the introduction of the County version, distinguishable by the side stripes on the body. Much to the joy of those using it, an acoustically damped interior roof trim was fitted, reducing noise levels as well as eliminating condensation dripping from the roof!

Although a little less classic than Series IIs, this last series of leaf-sprung Land Rovers make good sense for anyone looking for a good, usable Land Rover at minimal cost. They are a bit more comfortable than earlier ones, and definitely more pleasant to drive because of the better gearbox. Performance and economy are the same as the IIA's, and a late-model Series III, bought with care, can be used as everyday transport through the week, and for fun at weekends. Because these are the most recent of the Series models they are, generally speaking, in better condition than run-of-the-mill IIs and IIAs. Beware, though, because there are loads of decent-looking Series IIIs standing on top of badly rusted chassis, and powered by clapped-out engines, particularly diesels, which are driving through badly worn transmissions.

If you want a Series III with real performance – yes, honestly, it's possible –

Land Rovers must be inspected carefully before purchase, and the procedure should not be restricted to older models, such as this Series III. Range Rovers from the mid- to late-1980s and earlier Defenders can have serious rust and mechanical problems.

there's a version which might appeal. It's the so-called Stage 1, the first major development following huge government investment in Land Rover in the late 1970s, and it brought the mighty Range

Rover V8 engine into an otherwise fairly standard Land Rover. The engine was detuned from the Range Rover set-up (which in turn was detuned from its saloon car configuration) and was fitted only to long wheelbase models from early-1979, although British customers had to wait until the following year. It had the same permanent four-wheel drive transmission as used in the Range Rover, along with a lockable centre differential, improving the vehicle's load-carrying, towing, and off-road ability very considerably.

In fact, the V8 not so much improved but transformed the 109, and was the initial step towards the first of the modern, Defender-type Land Rovers. Indeed, the Stage 1 looks somewhat like an early 110. It had been found necessary to reposition the set-back grille flush with the wings in the style of models yet to come, giving the first V8 a completely different identity to the vehicle on which it was based.

Although a high proportion of Stage 1 production was exported, enough have survived in Britain to make them an alternative to the more conventional Series III. The big attraction, of course, is the V8 engine and the permanent 4×4 transmission, which, together, are a massive improvement on the more normal 4-cylinder petrol/diesel engines and their selectable four-wheel drive transmission. But there's a huge price to pay in fuel consumption. The Rover V8, like all V8s, is not particularly fuel efficient, and in this re-worked Series III it was at its thirstiest, with something like 10–14mpg in normal use.

Another drawback is that, apart from the engine and transmission, the vehicle was entirely series III, with the leaf springs, relatively poor steering, and basic cabin which so characterised the Series vehicles. But if you are drawn to the Series III because of its close connection with the original Land Rovers, but want more power, you'll do no better than a Stage 1. Buy some Shell shares first, though!

Range Rover (1970–96)

It's an interesting fact that the Range Rover was introduced a year before the Series III, and that because of this Land Rover had a thoroughly modern machine in production for a full 13 years before the utility vehicles were brought up to date with the launch of the One Ten, which, anyway, was essentially a Range Rover with a different body.

It has been stated elsewhere in this book that the importance of the Range Rover cannot be stressed enough. It was a vehicle genuinely ahead of its time and would be destined to remain the benchmark against which all other 4×4s will be measured right through to the turn of the century and beyond. It is, in my view, the best vehicle Land Rover have produced, and has attracted its own enthusiast movement, which is perhaps only equalled in dedication and fervour by devotees of Series I.

Range Rovers are all things to all people. They provide the ultimate in family transport, with ride and comfort levels in the luxury limousine category, but with massive luggage space thrown in, and the ability to tow the largest caravan or heaviest horse-box without effort. In addition they are increasingly being used by off-roading enthusiasts. Any Range Rover is a highly competent off-roader in standard form, but when you modify the wheelarches to take larger tyres and cut away the rear end in bobtail fashion it is as good on the rough stuff as a 90. Couple all these attributes with the low price of older models, and it is easy to see why the Range Rover is so popular. Good examples of late four-speed types can be

Perhaps the most suitable Range Rover for most people with the cash to spare is the 4.0 SE, which gives better economy than the 4.6 but is faster and has better towing ability than the 2.5 diesel.

found for between £1,500 and £2,000 at the time of writing, while early five-speeders (from 1983) are around £2,500 or less. The 3.5-litre engines gained fuel injection for the 1986 model year, but even these, with their greater reliability and slightly better economy, can be bought for about £3,000.

There have been two factory alternatives to the V8. An Italian VM 2.4 diesel engine was used for the Turbo Diesel model from 1986, upgraded to 2.5 litres in 1989, and then Land Rover's own 200 Tdi, pioneered with the Discovery, replaced the slightly more powerful VM with the 1993 model year. Furthermore, a great many owners have fitted their own diesel conversions over the years in order

to overcome the heavy fuel costs of the V8. In practice it is questionable whether the high cost of buying and installing a non-standard diesel makes any kind of sense financially (how many miles do you have to do to offset in fuel savings the £2,000–£4,000 price of an engine conversion?), and many conversions simply have not suited the vehicle. For example, some very low revving commercial engines have been used, giving the recipient vehicle a top speed of 60mph (96kph) or less!

If you're buying a Range Rover for off-road fun there's little point in paying a lot, especially if the cutting, grinding and welding equipment is going to be brought out of retirement. However, it makes no sense at all to buy the cheapest you can find if it's to be used as an everyday vehicle. Instead, buy the very best you can afford, paying more attention to overall condition than to year of manufacture and level of equipment. As to whether a 3.5 V8, VM diesel or Tdi is best, it really depends on what you intend to do with the vehicle and whether your pocket can tolerate the V8's fuel consumption, which will rarely, if ever, exceed 22mpg, and can be as bad as 15mpg if your driving involves lots of town work or your right foot is particularly heavy. The VM and Tdi can both give 27–30mpg, but neither have the sheer 'grunt' which makes the V8 such a delightful engine. Maximum speed suffers and the diesels can't get near the 100mph (161kph) that 3.5 Range Rovers can manage; acceleration, too, can only be described as sluggish with the diesels.

Range Rovers changed remarkably little throughout the lifetime of the original version, dubbed the Classic towards the end of its production, when the new version was also available. The shape didn't change at all, other than acquiring a second set of doors in 1981. The three-door models have particular appeal because they resemble most closely the 1970 vehicles with which it all began, but the five-door versions are undoubtedly more versatile, especially for family motoring. They began to acquire more creature comforts from the first of the In Vogue models of 1981, when the distinctive alloy wheels first appeared, and then improved progressively until by the time the fuel injection Range Rovers came along in 1986 they were quite sophisticated.

As a committed Range Rover enthusiast my own preference is for the five-speed models up to 1986, or one of the early four-speed automatics which became an option at the same time as injection came in. These are perhaps the best value

Range Rovers around these days, yet had not gone over the top in terms of luxury – something which was slightly to lessen the vehicle's appeal in the eyes of many enthusiasts as the Range Rover went ever more up-market.

The V8 moved up to 3.9 litres in 1989, and the 4.2 Vogue LSE became an (expensive) option in 1992, with such refinements as air suspension and traction control. But the writing was on the wall for the original Range Rover, which became badged as the Classic from September 1994 in order to avoid confusion with the new Range Rover, launched at the same time. Retrospectively, many people now refer to all original-shape Range Rovers as Classics.

The new Range Rover took over where the original had left off, ascending to quite amazing heights of electronic sophistication, much to the dismay of enthusiasts, most of whom are concerned about the practicalities of running them when they become older vehicles. Sticking with enthusiasts, the 4.0 and 4.6 versions make the most sense because the 2.5-litre six-cylinder BMW diesel engine simply does not have the right sort of power to propel the very heavy Range Rover and a caravan or horse-box with any sort of enthusiasm, and is not at all suited for off-roading.

However, it cannot be disputed that the new Range Rover is the best vehicle ever produced at Solihull, and provides a vivid demonstration of British motor manufacturing and design at its very best.

Discovery (1989–98)

The Discovery is an excellent vehicle and justly deserves the great success which is self-evident in towns and villages, motorways, country lanes, and supermarket car parks throughout the British Isles. Other than some transmission shortcomings it has absolutely no design faults, although countless owners can tell horror stories about problems caused by Land Rover's great weakness, poor quality control. These difficulties were thrown into stark relief because the Discovery was a new product aimed at a sophisticated and demanding sector of the motoring public. The problems were no worse than Defender customers have always put up with, as indeed have the purchasers of Land Rovers since 1948, but the situation was unacceptable on an expensive, up-market machine. And yet the company seemed determined not even to recognise that there were difficulties.

The faults included leaking roofs, windows and doors, poor finish, premature rusting, and problems with switchgear and minor controls. However, the Discovery is so good – and has become so much better as time has progressed – that very few owners have regretted their choice.

The only problems which have really let it down have been connected with the main gearbox. Again, it is not a matter of design because the box itself is very good, but one of unreliability in some of the components. These difficulties can cause problems ranging from poor gear selection, jumping out of gear, excessive noise, and even total loss of drive. But to put this into perspective, there are a great many Discoverys with satisfactory gearboxes for every one with problems, and the faults have been far less frequent with the completely new gearbox introduced along with the 300Tdi engine. Quite simply, the Discovery is easily the best machine of its type, and nothing that any other company – European, American, or Far Eastern – has ever produced can be considered as a true competitor. It is extremely closely related to the Range Rover, being built on virtually the same

Enthusiasts with a love of off-roading, or a desire to stand out from the crowd, are often tempted by the many Camel Trophy Discoverys on offer at specialist dealers. The winch can be useful too.

chassis, with the same kind of running gear, transmission and suspension, yet has a unique character.

Not surprisingly, the Discovery comes over as a much more modern machine than even the run-out Range Rover Classic, and is a very different vehicle to drive, even when powered by the good old V8, which gives it quite outstanding performance. Most Discoverys, of course, are diesel powered, and despite the size and weight the performance is more than acceptable with both the 200Tdi and 300Tdi units, although the latter is quieter and just a little smoother. Expect 27–32mpg on average with the Tdi, but little more than 20mpg with the V8.

Like the Range Rover, the Discovery is enormously versatile. Both will carry five adults in comfort, plus their luggage, and both make excellent tow vehicles. Discovery owners wishing to carry large loads find that with the rear seats folded down the high roofline provides exceptional load space.

110, 90 and Defender (1983–)

The very first working Land Rover to have coil spring suspension was the One Ten (the figures 110 and Defender name were to come later), introduced in 1983. It was based on an extended and strengthened version of the Range Rover chassis and used Range Rover coil spring suspension all round. It could have been pro-

If you want a 90 which is something special, you could do far worse than something like this one built by E. H. Douglas, near Banbury, Oxfordshire, with a 3.9-litre V8 engine, air suspension, and automatic transmission.

duced years before, but Land Rover was concerned about the reaction of many of its customers around the world to a more sophisticated working vehicle and, being a relatively small company with limited development funds, could only progress at a slow pace.

Most outstanding version of the original One Ten was that powered by the V8 engine, using the identical four-speed gearbox and transmission arrangement from the Range Rover. But it was also offered with the tried and tested 2.25-litre petrol and diesel engines, both of which were given five gears. These first One Tens had Series III type sliding side windows for the cab, yet a curved, one-piece windscreen in place of the earlier model's split screen. Sliding windows apart, they were a huge advance.

Find one of these today in good condition and you've a classic – moreover, a classic capable of hard use and sufficiently different from the succeeding Defender machines to help you stand out from the crowd. Best version is the V8 but, as with the Stage 1 V8, be prepared for very frequent visits to fuel pumps. I had one of the very early V8 110s when it was about three years old, and it was the thirstiest vehicle I have ever owned, or would want to own, but boy, it sure had character!

The first Ninety came along a year later. The development work consisted of little more than scaling down the 110, but it was set to develop in turn into the

The standard 90 hard-top is such a good vehicle that it is sometimes difficult to relate it to the spartan, underpowered, and thirsty utility vehicles from which it is descended.

Defender 90, the most hard-working and competent 4×4 of all time. The 90 – or when talking about earlier models, the Ninety – brought winding windows and optional cloth seats into the line-up, although strangely it was available initially with only the four-cylinder petrol and diesel engines which were optional to the One Ten's V8. The Ninety V8 came later. But the Ninety showed its capabilities straight away, having a level of off-road ability which exceeded that of the One Ten. Again, as with the One Ten, if you can find one of these early Ninetys in good condition, not an easy task these days, you're buying a piece of motoring history.

From this point the utility Land Rovers progressed in leaps and bounds. The now venerable diesel was very soon increased to 2.5 litres, but with only 68bhp it was still not up to the mark, and then in early-1987 it acquired a turbocharger. This took maximum power to 85bhp, but so good was the development work that maximum torque came at 1,800rpm. The Turbo D, as it was called, was the first true transformation of diesel Land Rovers and, despite what some critics might tell you, it is a first-rate unit capable of giving long, reliable service provided it is properly cared for. Neglected servicing, though, can lead to trouble.

I had the use for some time of the 1987 Turbo D 90 which was *Land Rover Owner* magazine's 'office' vehicle after buying it for the magazine from the Independent Land Rover Centre in Huddersfield. We did what many owners do, modifying the vehicle from a basic hard-top to a County-type machine, fitting it with forward-facing rear seats and B. F. Goodrich Mud Terrain tyres. The rear seats were not used very much – there just isn't the space in the back of a 90 – but the tyres, engine, transmission, and suspension were tested to the limit in countless off-road

expeditions. It showed me what can be done with a relatively inexpensive Land Rover, proving that even today the Turbo D is a viable option for anyone wanting the versatility and good looks of a 90 at minimum cost. Buy a basic one and customise it to your own taste, as we did, and the enjoyment is even greater.

The final major step forward came in 1991 when, amid some controversy, the 90 and 110 gained the Defender name and, much more importantly, were given the 200 Tdi engine developed initially for the Discovery. Although related to it, this engine was a considerable improvement over the Turbo D, with better performance, better economy, less vibration and less noise, although direct injection diesels can never be as quiet as some indirect injection units. If you want the ultimate off-roader, this version of the 90, or the later 300 Tdi, are the ones to go for. That first Tdi engine actually produced just a little more torque than the V8, and with its instant throttle response (when using low ratios), excellent engine braking (for nasty descents), and lack of water-vulnerable electrics, it was the perfect off-road engine until, almost unbelievably, the 300 Tdi proved to be even better.

Even a heavily loaded 110 Tdi will cruise all day at 75mph (121kph), although hills haul the speedo back quite rapidly, which means that any Tdi-powered Land Rover can be used for everyday motoring, even if regular long journeys are involved. It is the first four-cylinder Land Rover (apart from the Turbo D) to be genuinely unafraid of motorways, and the first to be able to approach 30mpg in general use. Who could ask for more?

RIGHT The versatility of the Discovery has made it one of Britain's most popular vehicles, and the market-leader in its category. It makes an excellent choice for families requiring a mixture of luxury car, load-carrying estate, and weekend off-roader.

Buying a Land Rover

Because of the considerable similarity between all vehicles produced by Land Rover, much of the buying advice applies fairly well across the entire range. A couple of important points to bear in mind are that buyers' expectations always have to relate to vehicle age, and that originality is important if you're even half inclined towards the classic side of the movement.

The most important component of any land Rover is the chassis, and careful inspection should be made to ascertain its condition. It would be unreasonable to expect the chassis of a Series II to be as good as that on a late Series III, because age inevitably takes its toll. However, your reaction to what you find depends on how the vehicle is being marketed, so a 'fully restored' vehicle of any age should have a chassis in excellent condition; if it has areas of rust, or badly executed repair sections, then it cannot be considered to be 'fully restored'. And don't think that because you're looking at a mid-1980s Range Rover there's no need to inspect the chassis. Although the Range Rover chassis was tough, it is not unknown for very serious rust to have developed by the time vehicles are 12–15 years old. Again, if the price reflects the true condition of the vehicle, and you take this into account, you may still end up with a good-value vehicle after paying for repairs. But please don't fall into the trap of buying without proper inspection, say, a 1984 Range Rover which you believe to be rust-free, only to find the chassis is rotten when you get it home.

Along with the state of the chassis, it is important with Series vehicles generally to check the condition of the springs, their hangers, and the chassis mounting points. Broken leaves can go unnoticed (or more likely ignored) by owners who 'forget' to inform prospective buyers; replacing them is not terribly expensive, but it's better that you don't have to. The suspension of coil sprung vehicles is not immune to trouble, either, and it is important to make sure that the vehicle sits squarely on the road, that there are no broken coils or badly rusted mounting areas, and that the dampers are doing their stuff.

Land Rover steering boxes are tough, but if badly worn will need replacing, although slackness in the steering is more likely to be caused by worn ball joints, bushes, or other components in the steering and suspension. The steering swivel joints are crucial, and should be inspected closely with the steering turned first one way and then the other. With time they get pitted and scored, which in turn prevents the seals doing their job, leading to loss of lubricant, which results in wear to the constant velocity joints. A little surface pitting is normal on older vehicles, but deep scoring, holes, and rust spell trouble.

Don't be alarmed at the amount of body roll when test driving a Range Rover, because it's a characteristic and not a fault. But what you should do is find a clear road and, at modest speed, turn the steering a little from side to side. The vehicle should roll generously, recover and then roll the other way as the movement changes, but should always feel controllable. If there's a sensation of rear-end steering there's suspension wear which requires correcting.

Older Range Rovers can develop pronounced transmission wear which spoils the enjoyment of the vehicle, and can make stop-start driving in heavy traffic a real pain. Test it by driving slowly in first gear, lifting the throttle and then accelerating; there will be some snatching, but if it's pronounced and uncomfortable it needs sorting. Expect gear whine on older Range Rovers, too – they all do it.

Check that the transmission is working properly on all Land Rovers, Range Rovers, and Discoverys. Series Land Rovers have selectable four-wheel drive as well as optional low ratios through the transfer box, all of which is controlled by the additional two levers located near the main gear lever. To engage four-wheel drive push down the yellow-knobbed lever (first engaging the locking mechanism of the front hubs if they're of the free-wheel type). Low ratios are selected by pulling back the red lever; as it comes back to engage low ratios the yellow lever should then spring up (if you have pressed it down), because four-wheel drive engages automatically when low range is selected with the red lever. The yellow lever is only likely to be used if four-wheel drive in high ratios is needed to help get across wet fields, or if snow or ice are restricting grip, but both should work as intended.

Land Rovers with permanent four-wheel drive have a separate, shorter gear lever to select low ratios which, when moved to the left (in the high or low positions), also locks the centre differential. On some older vehicles the low ratio position may be difficult to engage. This is sometimes a good sign because it can indicate that it has not been used, because the vehicle has not been off-roaded. Make sure it does engage low ratios, and check that the differential lock indicator light comes on when the lock position is selected.

Engines

Not all the engines used in Land Rover vehicles are as tough as legend would have you believe. Most durable of the lot are the two-and-a-quarter petrol engines used on leaf-sprung models; these units are surprisingly immune to neglect and will soldier on for years with just the occasional check on oil and water levels. However,

treat one properly and it will probably outlast all the modern engines.

When buying, listen for undue mechanical noise, and look for oil and water leaks, and blue smoke from the exhaust. Smoke, as everybody knows, is an indicator of internal wear (valve stem seals and piston rings are the likeliest causes), but countless smoking engines have continued to serve for years. The biggest worry is not that major failure is imminent, but that it won't pass the emissions test at the next MoT.

The older diesels are less long-lasting than their petrol counterparts, which is unusual, and they are prone to wear-related difficulties with the injectors and injector pump, as well as bottom-end problems. They are less powerful than the petrol units, incredibly noisy, and only a touch more economical (mainly because they're working that much harder all the time). Be wary of buying an older diesel if the engine is issuing blue, white, or black smoke, because it may well require expensive treatment, and will almost certainly fail the MoT.

The turbo diesels which are found on many older 90s and 110s are good units and, provided they've been serviced properly at the recommended intervals and have not been subjected to over-abuse, will often go on way past 100,000 miles before requiring major attention. It's much the same with the Tdis, although these are even more dependent on proper servicing and the use of correct oil types. However, it is worth bearing in mind that the average Tdi with more than 100,000 miles on the clock is probably going to require at least a top-end overhaul before too long, and a reconditioned turbo at the same time.

Be careful when buying a high-mileage diesel Discovery which has been used as a company vehicle. Normally, company-owned cars are a good bet because

The Freelander is an excellent vehicle, and is particularly good with a diesel engine. It is more like an everyday, quality car to drive than any other Land Rover, but don't expect it to perform off-road as well as a Discovery.

they've been properly serviced, but many Tdi Discoverys which have spent their first three or four years on a company's books have been driven flat out almost continuously. Too many people buy Discoverys because of their image, only to be disappointed with their performance compared with the Volvo, Ford, or BMW which came before. Consequently the poor Discovery is regularly revved to the maximum in each gear and cruised with the throttle on the floor, and engines will only take so much of this. Incidentally, this is why so many people complain about poor fuel consumption with Discoverys. Driven considerately, a Tdi Discovery will give about 30mpg, but used in the manner of a Formula 1 car you'll be lucky to get above 23mpg.

Even the mighty V8 is not immune to premature wear. The biggest problem with this engine, especially in its original 3.5-litre form, is that owners miss out on oil and filter changes as the engines get a bit older. This causes the oilways to sludge up, reducing oil feed throughout the unit. The most commonly affected component is the camshaft, which sits in the vee between the two cylinder banks, and is lubricated only by splash feed; reduced oiling is inevitable when servicing is neglected, and it is not unusual for cams and associated components (valve gear and timing chain) to need replacement at 70–80,000 miles. However, a V8 which has been properly serviced throughout its life, and where high-quality oils and filters have been used, can go on for 175,000 miles or more without requiring major attention.

The lesson is simple – try to buy V8 vehicles with service records, and check around inside the oil filler cap for signs of sludge or congealed oil. Also, listen carefully for noises from the camshaft, timing chain and tappets, with the engine both cold and hot; the tappets are hydraulic, and may rattle a bit for the first second or two after starting from cold, but if tappet rattle persists it is almost certainly an indication of neglect and wear.

Index